"I heartily recommend this book to anyone who wonders how generations of Catholics celebrated Christmas before the days of television and the mall, and anyone interested in living and passing on to the next generation a traditional heritage of Advent and Christmas centered on Christ."

— John Mallon, *The Sooner Catholic*

"Anyone using this delightful and moving book during Advent will experience great graces. The Baroness holds up a mirror to help us see ourselves, to listen to our own hearts, to open our minds to thoughts that speak to the spirit within reminding us always to be humble, attentive, caring. . . . An excellent gift."

— Fr. James Gray, OSB, *The Prairie Messenger*

"Reading *Donkey Bells* . . . is a beautiful way to prepare for the holy season of Christmas. It includes meditations to prepare our hearts, stories, customs and traditions celebrated during Advent and Christmas. This book is a treasure guaranteed to be used each Christmas as we prepare in our homes to celebrate Christ's birth."

— Mary de Marco, *The Bread of Life*

"*Donkey Bells* is a delightful collection of Advent and Christmas readings . . . it provides inspiring and intriguing thoughts on this most 'expectant' of Christian seasons. . . . This charming 'three-in-one' book will delight you and also makes a terrific Advent gift."

— Br. Larry Holley, OSB, *The Pecos Benedictine*

Donkey Bells

Advent and Christmas
Stories, Traditions and Meditations

with

Catherine de Hueck Doherty

Compiled and edited by
Mary Bazzett

Also includes:
The Christmas Angel O'Ryan by Eddie Doherty
The Bruised Reed by Jude Fischer

MADONNA HOUSE PUBLICATIONS

COMBERMERE • ONTARIO • CANADA • KOJ 1LO

www.madonnahouse.org

Copyright © 2000 Madonna House Publications. All rights reserved.
No part of this book may be reproduced, stored in a retrieval system, or transmitted in any form or by any means, electronic, mechanical, or otherwise,
without written permission of Madonna House Publications.

Cover painting by Heidi Hart

Design by Rob Huston

Third printing, November 21st, 2000
Feast of the Presentation of Mary

Printed in Canada

Canadian Cataloguing in Publication Data

Doherty, Catherine de Hueck, 1896-1985
    Donkey bells : Advent and Christmas

ISBN 0-921440-38-3

1. Advent—Meditations. 2. Christmas—Meditations.
I. Bazzett, Mary II. Title

BX2182.2D64 1994   242'.33   C94-900563-0

This book is set in Bodoni, designed by Morris Fuller Benton in 1908–15, and
based on typefaces designed by Giambattista Bodoni of Parma, Italy, at the end of
the eighteenth century. Headings are set in Galahad, designed by Alan Blackman
as a cross between Optima and the flat-pen writing of Friedrich Neugebauer, the
distinguished Austrian calligrapher.

Contents

Book I — Meditations

Book II — Customs and Feasts

Book III — Stories

Foreword

A wisp of wood smoke curls lazily into the cold, clear sky near the little village of Combermere, Ontario. It is November, or perhaps December, and the members of the Catholic lay community founded by Catherine Doherty are observing Advent and, soon, the Christmas season. It is a warm, family time for them. The winter chill outside, amid pines and birches on the Madawaska River, contrasts with the toasty warmth of the buildings inside. There is a sense of quiet expectancy. It is a peaceful, hope-filled time of waiting until the holy feast of Christ's birth is celebrated. A joyous Twelve Days of Christmas follows, giving festive expression to the miracle of the Incarnation.

The hiddenness of Nazareth prevails at Madonna House, as the simple joys of Jesus' coming are celebrated. Without the glitz and glitter of commercialism, it is easier to find the essence of the holy season. The community members live the Gospel as their foundress taught them, in humble, poor surroundings, depending on donations from benefactors for clothing and other necessities. Yet their hearth and hearts are open in hospitality, hosting dozens of guests for the Christmas holidays.

In the following pages, you will read how Madonna House prepares for and celebrates Christmas, from the words of Catherine to her staff, as well as through seasonal customs and traditions. It is my hope that you will bring some of these traditions into your *own* home, wherever you may be. In the city or country, with a large family or living alone, there are ideas and meditations here that are shared to enrich your walk with Christ. They are ways to 'enflesh' the Gospel, as Catherine would say.

Enfleshing the Gospel was what Catherine de Hueck Doherty's life was all about. Born in 1896 to a wealthy family in Old Russia, Catherine learned from her mother's knee to live the Gospel. She learned that to serve the poor was a privileged way to touch Christ, and she never forgot it.

She touched Christ and served Him during her days as a nurse to the Czar's troops during the Russian Revolution. As a young bride, she and her husband, Baron Boris de Hueck, fled communist Russia, losing their wealth and prestige. As refugees in Canada, Catherine worked at menial jobs to help support her ailing husband and their infant son.

Eventually, she found work with a lecture bureau and became wealthy once again. Yet she felt that God was calling her to give up her money and possessions, to become poor, voluntarily, for His sake. She and her husband went their separate ways and their marriage was later annulled by the Church.

Catherine followed the impulse of God to "sell all you possess." She provided for her son, and then, with the blessing of her bishop, she gave the rest of what she had to the poor. Then she went to live in the slums of Toronto, to pray and beg and to help people in small, humble ways.

What grew from her obedience to God was Friendship House, an apostolate of lay people who served the poor. It eventually expanded to help the poor in New York City's Harlem section, in Chicago, and in other cities and towns of North America.

Catherine became a pioneer in Catholic Action and social justice work, for which she received both awards and accolades, as well as insults and injuries by racists. She was a friend of Dorothy Day and also of Thomas Merton, who spent part of a summer working with her in Harlem.

During this time she was interviewed by newspaper reporter Eddie Doherty, who promptly fell in love with her. As it turned out, the attraction was mutual, and, upon promising to her bishop that Catherine's apostolate to the poor would always come first, Eddie married Catherine.

Eventually, the couple went to Canada to extend the Friendship House movement. They worked with the rural poor and established Madonna House. Their tiny apostolate attracted lay people and, later, priests. Today it numbers some 200 full-time members (including about 20 staff priests) plus another 100 or so associate clergy. There are more than 20 field houses across North America and sprinkled throughout Europe, Africa, South America, the Caribbean, and even Catherine's native Russia. Each field house was established at the request of a local bishop. The service of each house varies, from busy soup kitchens to quiet houses of prayer.

Madonna House is a 'public association of the faithful,' established according to canon law and approved by the Catholic Church. Each member of Madonna House makes promises of poverty, chastity and obedience, and wears a simple silver cross engraved with the words *pax* and *caritas*— Latin for peace and love.

In the holiday season of 'peace on earth'—and love—the message of the Gospel becomes especially clear at Madonna House. Catherine might say that it is as clear as the bell of the little donkey, carrying Mary to Bethlehem with Joseph. She always said the donkey's bell was the first church bell.

If you listen closely, you can almost hear that first church bell, along with the little donkey's hooves on the cobblestones of Bethlehem. The way Catherine talked about Bethlehem and the cold cave and the straw of the manger, her listeners could almost see it, almost touch it. The Good News was incarnated, in Christ and also in Catherine, in her life and in her words.

As you read now, imagine yourself listening to her words as she speaks to you. Join with the Madonna House staff for a cup of tea, and listen as she talks about Advent and Christmas. Join the staff as they gather to decorate, or prepare for Mass, or celebrate the feast days of the season. Imagine the aromas of spicy gingerbread baking and pungent pine decorations. Bring your loved ones along, and listen as Catherine tells stories of her girlhood home in Russia or of her days working among the poor in Harlem; or listen to Eddie's incomparable yarn of an Irish angel. Listen as Catherine speaks to you through the pages ahead. Listen closely and you will hear the bell of the donkey. Listen, and learn the rich, varied traditions that are yours for the taking—yours as a believer in the God who came to earth, so humbly and so quietly—the God who, for our sake, became a human baby in a cave in Bethlehem.

Mary Bazzett

Book I

Meditations

Catherine Doherty was a woman of faith and prayer, who loved to talk about God and the things of God. During Advent, she spoke to her staff and guests to help them prepare their hearts for the Birth of Christ. She spoke about the Christmas season as well.

The following excerpts are from her daily talks to the Madonna House family during Advent and Christmas. Their tone is informal, yet serious, much the way you might speak to your loved ones about something important. Picture yourself now in the Madonna House dining room after dinner, as Catherine begins to speak to you.

The Meaning of Advent

Advent is a strange word. It means 'coming'. An advent is something that is 'arriving soon'. When we have something coming, when we expect an event, an advent, we are usually alert inside. We are listening. My family is coming for Christmas and I am in the country, and I am listening for the sound of a car. It is a special car, and I am filled with a special listening.

Advent is such a beautiful season. It is a time for renewal; it is especially a time for forgiveness because God brings His forgiveness to us in the shape of His Son. The Church year begins with the first Sunday of Advent. And every time it comes around, my heart thrills anew.

For me, the word 'advent' has a double connotation. It means the arrival of a new liturgical season, the preparatory time for Christmas, for 'the coming of Our Lord' as a Child on earth, for His incarnation in time. But it also means that *other* advent—the parousia, the second coming of Christ, in glory, at the end of the world. That is an advent which Russian hearts long for and expect. They hope it will happen in their lifetime, but, even if it doesn't, they rejoice that it will happen in someone else's lifetime.

These two Advents blend in my soul, mind, and heart. They bring a hunger and a longing that beggars words, for they are the seasons of *expectation*. Expectation of what? Of whom? To me, of the Tremendous Lover, of the Lord, Christ.

To me, the bells of this season, whenever they ring, either for Mass or for the Angelus, always have the joyous sound of wedding bells. For Advent is 'the springtime of love', when the soul awaits her Lover, knowing deep down that He is coming and that He will make her His own!

This knowledge is unshakable. It is based on a faith that is immovable, filled with a knowledge that is found, not in books, but in the prayer of silence, the prayer of love.

To meet this Lover, our Bridegroom, we must *be awake* for Him. In his letter to the Romans (13:11–14), St. Paul calls us in a loud voice to arise from our sleep! Our salvation is nearer than we believed; the night has passed, and the day is at hand. This call of his means *now!* Today! Every day of the year, every hour of every day is the hour for us to arise from our sleep.

We have so many 'sleeps'. We have that strange inner sleep that wants to escape from whatever we have to conduct in the marketplace with the powers of secularism. And we have that other emotional sleep that drags us into bed (literally, if we only could get there) to escape an even bigger fight with the powers of darkness within ourselves. For we know that we have to 'die to self' so that we may live in Christ, and this is hard for us to face.

We also have to fight the simple sleep of weariness that any vocation places on the shoulders of its members—weariness of body, weariness of mind, and weariness of soul.

Yes, St. Paul is right: we must arise from our sleep. Let us come out of the night of our emotions—the night of our anger, of our hostility, of all those negativities within us. Let us walk in the daylight of simplicity, of friendship, of forgiveness, of understanding, of tenderness and gentleness to one another.

Advent is a time for this *arising.* It is such a joyous season, such a loving season! Let us enter into its joy.

Advent in Old Russia

My mother used to say that the days of Advent were the days of building a golden stairway that would lead us to a star, the star of Bethlehem. And this, in turn, would lead us straight to the Christ Child!

In my youth, that stairway was real. Each day I could see and touch each step of it, as it was being built. The first steps were made of *cleanliness*. We began cleaning from the inside out.

First, there was the Advent fast: to clean the soul of all its past faults and sins, to make penance for them, to wash it with tears, and the heart with contrition.

As in Lent, all meat, milk products, eggs, and sugar disappeared from the family table, to be replaced with fish, vegetables, and honey. The parish church became the focal point of our daily lives, and church services dominated the day.

But there was a difference. In Lent, the Russian women donned dark garments, took off their jewelry, and allowed no music in the house for the forty sad, cruel days of the Lord's passion. Not so in Advent. On the contrary, there was talk of new clothing. There was a flurry of buying materials and of sewing. There was much music in the air, and the practicing of hymns and songs to be sung on the Holy Night. Even the fast itself was one of joyous expectation.

Masses, communions, confessions, and evening services in the church followed one another closely throughout the days. To accompany these inner preparations, outward cleaning and scrubbing went on feverishly all about the house, with everyone humming snatches from ageless tunes.

The first to be cleaned and polished were the icons, which shone and became alive under the flickering shadows of the votive lamps—red and blue and green. To my childish eyes, they were the forerunners of the lovely candles on the Christmas tree.

A Short Season—A Long Journey

Advent is a short season, yet it covers a long distance. It is the road of a soul from Nazareth to Bethlehem. It seems such a short distance as we are accustomed to thinking of distances. Yet it is a road into infinity, into eternity. It has a beginning, but no end. In truth, Advent is *the road of the spiritual life* which all of us must start if we do not want to miss the way.

We must start with a 'fiat' that re-echoes Mary's fiat ("Let it be done, O Lord"). It is a fiat that each of us should say in the quiet of our hearts.

Let us arise, then. Let us shake the sleep out of our eyes—the sleep of emotions run amuck; the sleep of indifference, of tepidity, of self-pity, of fighting God. Let us arise from that sleep with its dark nightmares, and begin our journey to Bethlehem.

But let us understand that this 'Bethlehem' we seek is *within* our own souls, our own hearts, our own minds. Advent is a time of standing still, and yet making a pilgrimage. It is an *inner* pilgrimage, a pilgrimage in which we don't use our feet. We stand still; yet, in a manner of speaking, we walk a thousand miles across the world—just because we choose to stand still.

So, then. Let us enter, you and I, into the pilgrimage that doesn't take us from home. For ours is a journey of the spirit, which is a thousand times harder than a journey of the feet. Let us 'arise and go'.

Our Lady's Pregnancy—and Ours

All of Advent, you know, is really Our Lady's Feast. Yesterday I was thinking about her pregnancy. She was told that the Holy Spirit would overshadow her. She was a virgin, and did not know any man, so she must have waited and then felt life within herself!

I thought of this fantastic situation—God imprisoned in the womb of a woman for nine solid months. Such a stupendous thought! It sort of 'blows' your mind. I said to myself, "What is it that we are lacking today?" (I included myself in this question.) And the answer came, "I think it is *the ability to be pregnant* with God."

Yes, that's it. For it wasn't Mary alone who was pregnant with Him. It's you and I who should be pregnant with Him. At baptism, our soul (or our heart, as we say) is opened to becoming pregnant with God. We have entered into His kingdom.

We're small; we're little; we don't understand much. But the years pass by quickly, and we begin to be faced with the reality of our baptism in Christ. And we say to ourselves (or we should): "Am I pregnant with Christ?" There is a period in our lives in which we *must* become pregnant, because pregnancy means growth.

Eventually, this Christ whom we have accepted into the womb of our heart is going to become a Child. And then He will grow and grow and grow—for *God needs room!* You see, having given birth to Him in faith, we must be ready for the next step: to become an Inn.

These are facets of Advent that are so immense that we can barely absorb them: to be a womb, to be pregnant with Christ, to allow Him to grow and to expand our hearts under His grace. These are thoughts we can meditate on for years.

Of course, if we allow Christ to grow in us, He, like the good Samaritan, is going to bring a lot of wounded people into the 'inn' of our heart. In fact, knowing the size of our heart, and being able to enlarge it (if we let Him) He will make our pregnancy become a fantastic gift to the world!

Think about it: becoming pregnant with Christ! You know, it shakes me. I don't know if it shakes you, but I was thinking of the incredible situation of God being welcomed into a human womb. And to do that, He needs our availability. He needs our emptiness.

Let me share with you what Caryll Houselander wrote about emptiness in her book *The Reed of God*, which is one of the best books on Advent:

> That virginal quality which, for want of a better word, I call emptiness, is . . . not a formless emptiness, a void without meaning. On the contrary it has a shape, a form given to it by the purpose for which it is intended.
>
> It is emptiness like the hollow in a reed, the narrow riftless emptiness which can have only one destiny: to receive the piper's breath and to utter the song that is in his heart.
>
> It is the emptiness like the hollow of the cup, shaped to receive water or wine.
>
> It is emptiness like that of the bird's nest, built in a round, warm ring to receive the little bird.

The pre-Advent emptiness of Our Lady's pur-
poseful virginity was indeed like those three things.

She was a reed through which the Eternal Love
was to be piped as a shepherd's song.

She was the flower-like chalice into which the
purest water of humanity was to be poured, mingled
with wine, changed to the crimson blood of love, and
lifted up in sacrifice.

She was the warm nest rounded to the shape of
humanity to receive the Divine Little Bird.

Yes, that's what Our Lady was, and that's what we must be
too. We must be all these things in order to receive the Child.

Meditate on this. Let an image assemble before your eyes
so that you can think of it. Slowly, your desire to know, your
urge to manipulate, will fall away like worn-out garments.
Many things will fall away. Then you will be empty, and able
to receive the incredible.

A Candle in Our Hearts

Advent is the time of expectation. True, Christ has already
come upon earth. He has been crucified, and has risen. He is
with us now, in His Church. And yet, somehow, as the season
for commemorating His birth approaches, something stirs in
us, something deep and profound, *as if we are expecting a
great miracle.*

As the Christmas season approaches, everyone feels a
certain 'something' that cannot be put into words. There are
no words that fit. We begin to realize that we are expecting
'something'—or 'Someone'—and we become a little bit more
aware of our insides, of a 'burning' in our heart.

We will find that it is like a candle within us. It is not a big candle. We must keep this flame alight, so that it burns through the layers of whatever we have put on top of it, and allow the expectation that is within us to come forth.

This is so important because, if we can burn away each layer that we have put on through the years, then we will be filled with joy. We will become full of gladness, knowing that a great gift is about to be given to us.

How much have we put into our heart, each one of us?

Advent—A Time of Faith

When you come down to hard brass tacks, Advent is meant to be the time of faith. Unfortunately, one of the things missing in the world is faith. Ask a Protestant, a Catholic, a Jew: "Do you *really* have faith?" Many wouldn't know what to say, if they were honest. Ask yourself now, do you have faith? Real faith? Really??

Your faith should be *unshakable*, like a tree standing near the water, as it says in Psalm One. Your faith should be like a light within your heart to light your path, and the path of your friends, and others around you.

True faith is profound, immutable, unchangeable. *That* is the faith of our fathers, the faith which has been given to us by God via the Second Person of the Trinity, Jesus Christ.

Now, stop a moment and ask yourself again: "Do I really believe?"

People come to Madonna House out of the blue. And I sometimes ask them, "Why did you come here?" They answer, "To see a Christian community." Well, isn't a parish a Christian community? And isn't there a Christian community around each and every person who really believes?

You know, if you wish to see a Christian community, you have only to look at yourself in the mirror. *You* are a Christian community! The Father, the Son, and the Holy Spirit (not to mention Our Lady, who's around the corner)—and you—form a community, or *should!*

Take a mirror and hold it up in front of your face. Is the person looking back at you really a Christian? That's something very easy to find out. How? In the old days, the pagans used to say: "Look at those Christians. How they love one another!" So, test yourself by asking some questions.

Do you love people? Old people? Ugly people? Beautiful people? Crippled people? All kinds of people? *Do* you? Would you give your life for any one of them? Christ said, "Greater love has no man than he gives his life for others" (John 15:13).

All you have to do is get a mirror! Look at yourself and ask yourself the question, "Do I live the Gospel without compromise?" If you do, then *you* are a community. That's all there is to it. Father, Son and Holy Spirit—and you—form a community because you choose to obey the law of God. And that makes a Christian community.

Do you have faith that Our Lady is coming? Do you hear the donkey's bells as she nears Bethlehem? Do you have faith in her pregnancy? Do you have faith that, on a certain day, the Child will come from her womb? And that this Child is God?

Are you in love with God? Do you really believe that God is in this woman who is Our Lady, and that her Child is God? Do you really believe that? Do you act towards your neighbor as if he or she were Christ? Christ said, "Whatsoever you do to the least of my brethren, you do to Me" (Matt. 25:40).

Is that your motto in life? Is the tree of faith in your life unshakable? Ask yourself those questions.

We are in Advent. We remember that a woman held in her arms a Child, and that Child was God. If we remember that, then we are givers of peace; we are lovers of the Beloved. We own Him through love. And He owns us! The most extraordinary thing in the world is that God loves you and me!

Do me a favor—if you ever doubt, look again in the mirror. And then, bowing low before it, sing an 'Alleluia' that can be heard everywhere. No one can be so ugly, no one so tragic, no one so miserable as not to be beloved by God. That's something extraordinary! Aren't you filled to the brim with this miracle? It is so great!

And the greater your faith, the deeper that miracle. Think about it. Dream about it. Ponder it. And slowly, as you do, even without noticing it, you will become a saint.

Turning Our Face to Christ

Once again, we are in Advent, which reminds us vividly, beautifully, of Christ's first advent in time. Even while He is coming, He is also with us now, in many ways.

He is with us in the tabernacle. Incredible Love that He is, He could not separate Himself from us. He also walks among us in all His priests. Through their hands, He multiplies Himself in the Hosts so that they can feed us with the Bread of Life—Himself. How immense must be His love for us!

Think for a moment. Allow a few moments of silence to interrupt your reading of this page. Try to comprehend the lavishness of God's love for us. Daily, millions of Hosts are given in Holy Communion to the faithful throughout the world. And each Host is Christ, coming in tremendous love to be united to each and all. Think about it now!

Let every day be the day of *beginning again*, of loving Christ a little more, of hungering for Him a little more, of turning our face to Him. To accomplish this, all we need do is to look at the person next to us.

We must never forget that we shall be judged on *love alone*. And that there is only one way to love God and 'prove it' to Him: by loving our 'neighbor', the person next to us at any given moment.

I repeat, turning our face and heart to Christ simply means turning to the one who is next to us at *this* particular moment in our life. If we do that, dearly beloved, we shall be saints.

Bells and Donkeys

It came to me, during these days of Advent, that I should share with you a custom which is not necessarily liturgical but which adds to the enjoyment of this lovely season. It has deep spiritual connotations; at least it did for our family, and for many others I knew when I was a young child.

When I was a little girl, my mother used to tell me that if I was good during this holy season of Advent—and felt sure that I wanted to offer my little acts of charity and obedience throughout Advent to the little Christ Child for a gift on His birthday—then sometime during Advent, at first very faintly and then quite clearly, I would hear bells. As she put it, *the first church bells*.

These were the bells around the neck of the little donkey that carried Our Lady. For mother explained that Our Lady carried Our Lord. And she was the temple of the Holy Spirit, the first 'church' as it were, since Christ reposed in her. And the donkey, carrying Our Lady and sounding his bells as he walked, had the first church bells.

Around the second week of Advent, mother wore a little bracelet that had tinkling bells. As she moved her hand I could hear them tinkle, and I got excited because I associated them with the donkey's bells.

As young as I was, my imagination would build up a lot of little stories about the trip of Our Lady from Nazareth to Bethlehem—stories which I would share with my mother, and which would spur me on to further good deeds and little sacrifices.

During the third week of Advent, mother's bracelet miraculously got many more bells on it. Their sound grew louder and louder as Christmas approached. It was wonderful.

My brother and I used to listen. Mother's bells were first around her wrist and then around her knee too. Then more bells, as it got closer to Christmas. We were really excited about them.

I introduced this little custom in Madonna House. During Advent, I wear a kind of bracelet that can be heard as I walk or move, in whatever room of the house I might be. The members of our family tell me that it spurs them on, even as it did me when I was a child, to meditate more profoundly on the mystery of Advent. // –7

Here at Madonna House, we have begun in these last few years to make a collection of miniature donkeys—of wood, glass, ceramics, rope, you-name-it. And we have an album of Christmas cards (which we save from the many we receive) that depict the donkey in the manger scene.

The presence of the donkey and the ox in Scripture is symbolic of the prophets who foretold the Incarnation. And also of the fact "that the ox and ass know their Master's voice, but Israel doesn't know the voice of God" (Isa. 1:3). So, you see, there is some spiritual foundation for my love for the donkey which brings such great joy to my heart.

I'm sure that, as a child, Christ rode on a donkey many times. And also as a man, of course. But 'officially' (from the Scriptures) we know of only two times: one was when the donkey carried Our Lady, who in turn carried God, from Nazareth to Bethlehem. The other time was when the donkey carried Christ into Jerusalem as the people laid palm branches before Him, proclaiming Him king.

Let us think for a moment: what kind of animal is a donkey? It is a beast of burden, the animal of the poor. Once again, the immense theme of poverty is illustrated in an animal. God chose the humblest, the smallest in status, because among the animals the donkey is considered very low. So God is teaching us a lesson here—a lesson of humility, of poverty, and of simplicity.

Have you ever seen a newborn donkey? Well, every donkey has a black cross on its gray fur, a marking which is especially noticeable just after it is born from its mother's womb. It gets less clear as the donkey matures, but still, it is visible. I share this fact with you to teach you to open your heart to the bells of the donkey that carried Our Lady and also carried God.

The breath of the donkey and the ox made the stable warm. So we meditate on several things at once: the poverty and humility of the donkey, which God chose and which should be our poverty and humility; and the breath of our love, which should warm God in our neighbor constantly.

Let us remember that the donkey also had no room at the inn. If Our Lady and St. Joseph had been accepted at an inn, then the donkey too would have been received and would have been handed over to someone to see that it got a good cleaning, a good rubdown after the long trip, and a good amount of food.

But neither woman, nor man, nor donkey had a place at the inn. So they went to live in a poor stable that wasn't too well prepared for animals, let alone as a decent habitation for human beings.

Now, another meditation comes to us. Think of the millions of people who are left homeless on our streets. Tragic is this situation. We, as apostles, must be very careful that we do not exclude anyone from the inn of our heart.

I pray that our heart, our soul, our ears will hear very clearly 'the bells of the donkey', not only in Advent but throughout the year. For whoever who is pure of heart and childlike shall hear the bells of the donkey ring in their life.

The First Church Bell

Whenever I think of the days gone by and of my childhood, I usually write a little poem about it. Today, I wrote one on the donkey:

> Is your heart quiet?
> Your mind at rest
> In Nazareth?
> Your soul as joyous
> As a child's
> Before a flower, or a toy?
>
> Then listen!
> It will take a while
> But you will hear
> The clearest sound
> Of the first church bell.
>
> You have to be
> Very quiet
> And full of peace.

The sound will
At first be slight—distant.
It will travel
Slow . . . slow . . . slow . . .
But then, quite suddenly,
It will sound clear,
As if it were
Quite near.

But if your joy
Is very great
Your soul all ready
Your mind a child,
Then you will see
A little donkey
Full of humility
With little bells
Around his neck!

The sound, so clear now,
Will take you in
And lift you up
And you will know
That God's first church bells
Were the ones a donkey wore
Around his neck!

Repentance—
Preparing a Way for the Lord

Chapter 40 of the Book of the Prophet Isaiah contains some of the most beautiful passages in Scripture. These prophecies are eternal. They were not just meant for the time of Jerusalem; they are meant for *now!*

So please, once more, let us risk looking in the mirror and seeing who we really are. Let us realize that we are wonderful in the sight of God, that He loves us so much He has sent His own Son to redeem us. Advent is the season in which we remember this anniversary of His coming. It is a time for us to understand what we are truly worth.

First, Isaiah tells us to be consoled; he also explains to us that all our sins are forgiven. And then comes another verse, saying, "Prepare in the wilderness a way for the Lord."

We know that our heart and mind often are a 'wilderness' where we are trapped. We try to go here, there, and everywhere in this chaotic, uneven inwardness. And we seem to get nowhere.

"Let every valley be filled in." How many valleys have we got? How many dark and strange places in our mind and soul in which we hide? All because we don't want to face what we know we should: the Law of the Lord.

"Let every mountain and hill be laid low." We have mountains. Not 'the mountain of the Lord' but others—mountains of all kinds of pleasures, all kinds of desires. They have to be laid low.

"Let every cliff become a plain, and the ridges, a valley." Now, if we were in the Holy Land, we'd see the physical topography—the strange hills, mountains, ridges and so forth—of that land. But in this passage, the prophet is describing us in symbolic terms. Yes, *us!*

We have a real situation in our inner landscape that we have to face. We have to *repent*, that's what it really means! Repentance is a 'turning around'. Repentance isn't simply apologizing, then going to confession and being forgiven. Oh no! Repentance is much more than that. It is an ongoing affair. To understand that which we know we *must* do, and then to really *do* it. *That* is repentance.

To put it another way: repentance is the incarnation of the Gospel in our life. Yes, we acknowledge that we have sinned before the Lord. Yes, we acknowledge that we have trodden the wrong path. Now we must turn our back to all of that, and move in the opposite direction! Otherwise, in a little while we will be telling the same story all over again—to another priest, or to the same priest—asking to be forgiven again.

Repentance means *change*. In a sense, it becomes a 'bulldozer' that we apply to our mind and soul to level the ridges, flatten down the mountains, fill in the potholes and ravines, so as to make a path for the Lord to cross the desert of our heart.

We need to pray to the Lord for this 'bulldozer' so that the rockfall and debris can be pushed away. God will do this for us, provided we stop the swirling dust of our own mutterings, the constant use of the pronoun 'I', our continual thinking that we are always right and someone else is wrong, our non-listening to our own brothers and sisters, or to our spouse and children.

The weight of listening, *really* listening to others, is heavy. That is why we need to pray for a spiritual bulldozer to make straight the ways of the Lord in our own heart.

Then God Himself might walk these paths, unencumbered. He can come into our hearts and do the listening there. He can listen to others through us, talk through us, understand through us, help through us. He can console those who come to us.

If the paths of our hearts were made straight, He would come running! He wants to be with us until the end of time, as He said in the Gospel, and He still desires to serve. And what better service could there be than to have 'a listening ear of God' within our hearts?

It is time for us to pray, dearly beloved, so that we may be able to listen to the hunger of others. Usually, other people don't want us to do too much for them. They simply want us to listen because *listening means love and friendship,* for which there is such a great hunger today.

Yes, to repent is to change. It is not just to acknowledge that we have done wrong. It is to turn our back to the wrong, and start doing the right—incarnating the Gospel. Christianity in the world today hinges on this living the Gospel.

The world today doesn't believe that Christ's teachings are of any value, because the majority of Christians do not incarnate them.

Take, for example, Reverend Martin Luther King. He "had a dream." He incarnated that dream, and he was killed because of it. He did the very thing that people *expect* a Christian to do: he incarnated his beliefs. Do we?

"Make straight the path of the Lord, a highway for our God across the desert. Let every valley be filled in, every mountain and hill be laid low. Let every cliff become a plain and the ridges a valley. Then the glory of our Lord shall be revealed."

This glory can be revealed in each one of us. How? It's awfully simple, in a sense. All we need do is just to stop our personality clashes, our judgmentalism toward one another, our mistrust of one another, our anger against one another, our hostility against one another. All we need do is to *begin to love one another* as Christ loved us. Then the pagans of today will say: "Well now, look at those Christians, will you?

They've really got something. See how they love one another!"

Turning now to the first chapter of St. Mark's Gospel, we read about St. John the Baptist "preparing the way for the Lord."

Every fresh coming of Christ into the world has followed the work of those who, in the spirit and in their lives, have been road-makers. Christ needs preparers of His way. We prepare the way of Christ whenever we give Him leverage in our life, a place in our life, in *all* of our life.

A receptive mind is an indispensable road-making tool. We make His path straight whenever we bring His word to a world that is dying for lack of it. We 'go before His face' and we 'make ready for Him' whenever we help to remove the things which block His entrance into our world: greed, pride, hatred, personality clashes, divisions among us. Nothing *less* than repentance can lead the world out of disaster today.

Human beings must be set in a new direction, turning away from their fatal scramble for power, prestige, advantage. In the forefront of John's call for repentance was his sense of the coming judgment. Ours is the day when the coming judgment cannot only be seen but felt. The noise of bombs going off in Ireland (and other troubled spots in the world) and the bitter cry of the widows and children are shouting clearly, right across the world: *Repent!*

Repentance is more than penitence. It is not remorse. It is not admitting mistakes. It is not saying in condemnation, "I've been a fool." Who of us has not recited such a dismal litany? All of us have. They are common and easy to recite. Repentance is *more*. It is even more than being sorry for one's sins. It is a moral and spiritual revolution!

To repent is one of the hardest things in the world; yet it is basic to all spiritual progress. It calls for a complete breakdown of our prideful self-assurance, a stripping away of the cloak of prestige that is woven from our petty successes, a breaching of the innermost citadel of our self-will.

The Alms of Loving Words

Almsgiving during this season can be in the form of money (which is the basic meaning of 'alms'); but it can also be in the form of giving food, or clothing, to others. Now, not everybody may be able to give these away, but all of us are able to give *the alms of words*, which we all hunger to receive.

We can give the alms of words everywhere. See that lonely child? That troubled teenager? Have you a moment to spare to give him the alms of a few little words? They will bring light into his darkness (which really should not be there). Making friends with those who are lonely, lost, or unloved—be they rich or poor—is to bring Christ to them. Take one individual into your heart, and you are taking Christ into your heart! Surely He will reverse the process in eternity by taking you into His heart!

Like all other alms, our words must be given to others lovingly, gently, thoughtfully, in union with Christ. Without these qualities, we prostitute the very act of giving. Alms given *without* love, compassion, graciousness or deep understanding bring only hurt and pain. They do even more damage than indifference and coldness.

Is our love ever-watchful, ready to give to others the alms of gentle words? Our spoken words may be like a 'key' that can keep a door from closing. A gate may be opened, allowing light and love to flood minds that are beginning to doubt the very existence of love.

Do our eyes really see? Are we not blind to the thousands of little signs that exist in our own family? Father is a little grayer, a little more worried, a bit more silent. Mother is more tense, often with eyes that reveal tears. Sister or brother is sharper, thinner, less pleasant, more withdrawn. Do we really see?

Are we convinced that we are our 'brother's keeper'? Do we understand how far this 'keeping' goes? Business associates, friends, fellow workers, neighbors, strangers who cross our paths now and then—our whole every-day world—*all* are our brothers and sisters, whom we must cherish in the Lord.

A smile and a pleasant word about the weather given to an ill-clad poor person in a public conveyance, or to a stranger anywhere, might mean the difference between their hatred for all that we stand for, and their understanding.

For example, with foreigners, clearly enunciated words, spoken slowly and lovingly, with a smile of encouragement, are rich 'alms'. The sick may be tiresome sometimes in their self-centeredness, pain and loneliness, their repetitious speech. They too need our alms of words. The forgotten, the unwanted, the lost, the rambling alcoholic, the neurotic, the borderline 'psycho'—would they be where they are if someone had given them the alms of words when they so desperately needed them?

Such words of love, compassion and patience soothe the burning wounds of exhausted minds. They are so easy to give, yet so often withheld. They assuage the loneliness of the elderly, bring peace and joy, make crooked ways straight and people feel wanted and loved again.

Let us lovingly show Christ to our brothers and sisters in the thousand ways of love's ingenuity, but especially in the alms of loving words!

Poverty and Prayer

We should start realizing what true poverty is. First and foremost, it is a realization of *who we are*. We are created by God; we are creatures of God who are totally dependent on Him. We are the 'anawim', the poor people of Yahweh, the little people who know that they are totally dependent, who 'lean' on God, knowing that without God they can do nothing. This is the first step to prayer—to know who we are: saved sinners, entirely dependent on God. We are *dependent*. To the proud, this is anathema. We look at ourselves and we say, "I depend on no one," and suddenly, in the very saying, we realize that we do. This is the beginning of prayer: that we become beggars before God, knowing that even the steps we take are given to us by God.

To begin to pray, then, is to first cleanse our souls of arrogance and pride. In grave humility and as beggars, we come to Him who alone can make us princes and kings and queens, not of earthly kingdoms, but of the kingdom of God.

When we are thus poor and realize our total poverty, then we can go to Bethlehem and meet the Child who became poor for us.

The Reality of Christ's Poverty

The Son of God and the Son of Man was born in a cave. Over the centuries we have sentimentalized it. It is time for us Christians of the 20th century to take another look at this cave, and at Him who was born in it. People who live in caves or give birth to children in caves are not the wealthy of this world. They are poor. He, the Son of God, *chose* to be born in poverty. What does it mean to us moderns, this strange lesson of God's birth?

Are our hearts filled with longing for Him who loved us so much that He was born in a cave, and (by dying on a cross) took upon Himself the burden and slavery of our humanity and our sin?

Do we desire to follow Him and to detach our hearts from all things that are not of Him, in order to be 'poor' in spirit and in reality?

Are we going to share with the hungry ones of the world—the replicas of the Child who had nowhere to lay His head—from our immense surplus? Or are we going to give of our necessity? Will we spend millions on gifts for the man or woman 'who has everything'? Or will we give to those who have nothing, in memory of the Child who was also God and was born in a cave for love of us?

Are we going to the cave like the shepherds, who were also poor? Or are we going once more to 'render lip service' to a Christ of our *own* making, whose cave we have embellished with clean straw? (His probably stunk as old straw stinks in stables.) Which is it going to be?

One Precious Gift

At night I come to You,
O Holy Child,
Beseeching of Your majesty
Just ONE gift for me:

The gift
Of making others see
Your poverty
Eternally renewed
In endless stables cold and dank
Across our fair and immense land.

Stables where
You are born again,
Again! In little babies,
Weak and small,
Whose mothers, hungry and cold,
Have not even
Swaddling clothes
To wrap them in.

That is why at night
I come to You, O Holy Child,
Beseeching of Your Majesty
Just ONE gift for me.

The gift of making others see
Your poverty.
For then my empty hands will know
The weight of gifts
Of silver and gold and frankincense
Which I can then exchange
For food, for clothing, and for wood
To clothe and feed and warm the poor,
Both big and small.

You alone know their plight.
The height, the depth,
Of their needs, their fears.
O little Babe of Bethlehem

Help me to make others see
Your utter poverty on earth,
So that they may bring gifts
to feed and clothe
Your Majesty.

Giving of Ourselves

Here is another mystery wrapped up in Advent: the call to 'give of oneself' as Our Lady did.

Oh, we're willing to give ourselves—for a little while. We don't mind doing good works—for a little while. We don't mind doing this and that, whatever can help the neighbor, not at a very big cost to ourselves—for a little while.

But that doesn't work out; that doesn't work out at all. Not before the Child in the manger! Look at the Child in the manger.

There, you will see the utter poverty of Jesus Christ, the utter gift of Jesus Christ to us, as a Child. Then our 'giving only a little' doesn't work out, not at all. What we really have to do is *to surrender*.

It is immaterial if you are a priest, a nun, a mother, a father, a single person, a career woman or whatever. Name it, it makes no difference. If you are a baptized Christian, you owe it to that Child who was born to save us all in that total poverty, to embrace 'total' poverty. And this 'total' poverty must be embraced from *inside*.

Let's face it. If you are the father of a family, you cannot squander the money that should go for the education (or whatever) of your children. There is a certain limit as to what you can do in this situation, because that's your job, that's what God has called you to be: a protector, a provider. But, even if you can't give away your money, you can give *yourself*. (Now, that's very difficult!)

What we have here is a strange sort of 'meeting', the encounter of a mystery with a mystery. There is a little Child, who is God. And there is a human being who wants to 'give totally' to the Other.

These two, who have given themselves so completely, meet. The human being *allows* the Child to enter his or her heart, and to make a manger there. And in that human heart, this Child would grow, grow to manhood.

Whoever gives of themselves in this way, they too will become the Child. They will grow and mature into Christ. They truly will be an icon of Christ.

This 'giving of self' is strange. It is like a restlessness within the heart. It is like waves beating on the shore. It is the man or the woman who says, "I cannot rest unless I really surrender myself to God." And so, eventually, they do.

Without changing their style of life, without changing their vocation, their inwardness (that 'something' which is inside of a human being and which seldom comes forth) cries out: "I want to be one with God." It is said that whoever desires God possesses God. And how much more so a person who really wants to give *totally* of self!

It's very difficult for me to explain what this giving of one-self means. It is a sort of a 'listening of a human heart' to the heart of others, to the needs of others, wherever they may be. It is a human heart that 'understands' what has to be done for others, whoever they are, wherever they may be. It is a beau-tiful thing, but it is so rare.

We get all emotional about Christmas. We 'shell out' our effort and our money, or what-have-you. Then comes January and February and March; and we have *forgotten* so many things. We've forgotten to listen to the needs of others.

This 'listening' should begin in your own family. For you, entering the mystery of God's surrender to human flesh means that you must enter into a profound surrender to your neigh-bor, in a sort of blind totality that never questions but is always *ready and available*.

This is what today is sometimes called 'witnessing'. It's not enough to stand at the corner of a marketplace and pro-claim that you're a Christian. (That won't attract any attention!) But if you *act* as a Christian, then people will follow you. Yes, for miles and miles and miles.

But you will find it very difficult to distinguish how exactly to act; for this, you need help. Your greatest help is prayer, prayer to learn what has to be done and to do it. That is the great gift of discernment. But it also is a gift of courage, of giving your example.

Back during the Depression, at Friendship House in Toronto, I had so many people come to me for Christmas cheer (you know, for food), that I had a long list. I went begging all over the place for them, and kindly butchers and grocers donated enough to fulfill the needs of about 400 or 500 people.

Then, about two days before Christmas, a little mother came to me. She'd been sick and her husband had abandoned her. She had six children, and asked me for something to give them to eat.

All I could do was to phone a very rich person, a friend of mine, and explain the situation. She said: "You can forget it, Katie. I'll attend to it." So Christmas came, and Christmas went, and I was wondering what this lady had given the family.

About a week later, the mother dropped in and said to me: "It was wonderful! We had turkey and celery and sweet potatoes and a big cake. You should have seen it. It wasn't a basket; it was *four* baskets! And there were toys for all the children, and candies. Oh, we never had a Christmas like that!"

Then she stopped, and tears came to her eyes. "You know, there is one sadness in my heart," she said. "A handsome chauffeur with a beautiful car brought the gifts. But the lady who sent the baskets wasn't there, and so I couldn't thank her."

So, here was this very rich woman who sent the family all the *things* she could think of; but she didn't send *herself*. And that made all the difference! It's little things that count, you know. Tiny things! The rich woman probably had a lot to attend to, herself, so close to Christmas. But there it was!

That is the essence of Advent, and of Christmas too. God gives Himself to us 'without a backward glance'. How well He knew that He was going to be crucified, and all the rest of it! But He arrived as a Child. That is total surrender, total giving. God let himself be 'attended to' by a woman. And what with all the little difficulties babies have, that was quite 'something'! This is another mystery to contemplate: to allow yourself to be manipulated.

Have you ever connected this insight with the Blessed Sacrament: the Child in the manger and the Blessed Sacrament in the hands of a priest? And lots of times, not a priest. Carried wherever man wants to carry Him. Given wherever man gives Him. Just like a child.

Advent has great mysteries to it. I ask you to think about Advent and Christmas with a prayer, because prayer is the key to the door of these mysteries. And it is a door worth opening.

Flowering Advent Hearts

We are in Advent. It is a very beautiful time, a quiet time, a very still time. It's a time when the poustinia of the heart has its full flowering, and the flowering is in your heart.

As you wash dishes, do the laundry, or go about your daily work, something comes within from you. I call it a 'flowering', but really it is an expectation. Flowers 'expect' to be in full bloom, by and by.

The flowers open! *Maranatha*! The Lord comes, and you begin to feel that, really, 'something' fantastic is happening. It all happens *inside* your heart, though. It's not something anybody tells you, as though you were listening to a lecture or something. No, it is your heart that is speaking to you. Listen to it!

Little Things

Advent is a time of 'little things'—quiet, peaceful things like washing dishes, or changing diapers, or filing correspondence—or hectic things like running from one meeting to another, answering telephones, dealing with uncouth or difficult people, facing hopeless situations in schools or churches.

All these daily duties can be precious gems for us, gold too heavy for us to bear, grains of incense that would cover the earth, *if only our hearts could touch His heart* and generously open themselves to *being loved by Him* and love Him in return.

Yes, these 'little things' are with us during this Holy Season, just as they are during the rest of the year. But at Christmas time, we know enough to become little and child-like in our hearts. (At least I hope we do!) And if we become very small—like a mongoose or a rabbit (or even smaller, like a mouse)—then we will come to have the heart of a child.

What would happen if a child knew that this Baby in the crib was Jesus Christ Himself? Where would the child go? This 'little one'—this rabbit/mouse/child—would just jump into the crib and say, "Make room for me." Now *that* is a child! Why don't we do the same? There is plenty of room in the crib, you know, provided we are little.

Awake—Hear—Walk

Advent is the time of little things.
Did you walk in the night
And behold the delight
Of rabbits, raccoons, porcupines and mongoose?

Did you hear them discuss
What each would do
To make the night
Of the Little Child bright?

Did you wake in the dawn of a wintry day
And hear a thousand birds twitter
And sing of the holiest things?
And rehearse, and rehearse
Their flight, their songs
At Bethlehem.

Did you walk in the day
In the snow-clad fields
Where mouse and tiny field things
Eat and play?
If you did, then you know
That they plan a caravan
To a cave, a manger, a Child.

Are you going with them?

St. Joseph and Hope

I was meditating on fear last night, and I came to the question of hope. It is said that "perfect love casts out fear" (1 John 4:18). So I said to myself, what is hope doing in that combination? And it took me quite a while to think this out.

I settled on Joseph, for some unaccountable reason. There was Joseph and there was his pregnant wife, and he had not touched her. He had a dream, and he had to believe in that dream, which was, in itself, an act of faith.

I wondered, "How much hope did St. Joseph have during those nine months?" He must have gone up and down, emotionally speaking, because he was human. I imagine he'd look at Mary and say, "Well, maybe that dream was right, after all." And I realized that, in a sense, he 'personified' hope for us in the nitty-gritty.

I said to myself, "Where does hope come in?" The world news is such that it seems every moment everything is falling apart. So where is hope?"

Slowly, I focused on the thing that really mattered—*the moment of beginning again*. And that's when I tied it in with fear. It should allay fear and it should kill fear. The world has always known that it was in the throes of evil. Human beings are free to choose good or evil, and that is why the Gospel is not fulfilled in us, because we say *no* to the Holy Spirit.

But with God, every moment is the moment of beginning again. And when we 'begin again' with God, we enter the valley of joy, of plenty, of honey, of bread, and of wine. We do so because, no matter what we've done or where we've been, we are not lost. With God, every moment is the moment for us to begin anew.

St. Catherine of Siena, who is my patron saint, was praying for a man who was condemned to death. Just before he was beheaded, he turned back to the Church; the trip between prison and scaffold was his beginning again.

A man we call the good thief, crucified next to Christ, asked God to please take care of him. And Christ said, "This very day you will be in my kingdom" (Luke 23:43–44). Between the speech of the thief and the speech of God, everything began again. Hope surged forth in the thief's heart, immense and all-embracing.

We say that people are hopeless—the old, the forgotten, the hungry. And so they are! But those of us who have produced this hopelessness are guilty of a terrible sin, for it is the almost unforgivable sin—to cause someone to lose hope in God. No matter what else happens, this must not happen!

In our search for reality, in our running away from fear (and all those other emotions we are battered with), we still can possess hope. If we stretch out our hand, it will come to us. And whatever may seem hopeless will be filled with light.

We consider ourselves as 'the children of production'. We busy ourselves so much with the struggle to *produce* things. But hope springs up in our hearts, reminding us that there is something more to life than production, that we are bigger than 'it', because we are of God. It is this hope within us that makes us see that our price is His Incarnation, His Life, His Death and His Resurrection.

Hope, like an avalanche or a sort of fire, enters into us and we are renewed. Hope is the 'sauna' of the Spirit; the Holy Spirit uses it to cleanse us from all our emotions, from whatever bends us down.

Yes, we may *say* that perfect love casts out fears. But do we *believe* it? It would be a very good intellectual exercise for us to repeat it, over and over, or to write it on a blackboard. Then maybe it would get into our hearts. For if we turn our face to Hope—look Hope in the eyes, as it were—our life will become very simple, because Hope always holds Love in the hollow of its hand.

Faith, while we live, also holds Love. But so does Hope, because Faith holds both Love and Hope. "Look!" Faith whispers. "It's not so tragic! Nothing is tragic in the Lord; every moment is the moment of beginning again."

Okay, so you have sinned. So you are in the throes of guilt, and it is tossing you around like a hockey puck. Guilt has you in its claws! You must look at that guilt and say, "Out—out—out—out—out!"

With God, every moment is the moment of beginning again! So all that guilt just shrivels up (or should), and begins to crawl away, right out of the door. If you really put hope into action, this will happen. Doesn't that really cheer you up? (It cheers *me* up!)

So you see, then, that guilt is an utterly useless thing to indulge in! So you're guilty! So I'm guilty! So we're all guilty! If we apologize to God (via confession or outside of confession)—just apologize—that moment will be a moment of beginning again.

A sin is a sin, yes! A sin is a sadness that we give to God! Who of us wants to make God sad? So once we take that sadness away from God, by apologizing, why should we think about it again?

With God, every moment is the moment of beginning again. Every moment is hope. There is only one thing that can stop hope. It is when we desire to do *our* will instead of God's will. Very dangerous. Very. That is what happens when people say they want to 'do their thing'. Well, believe me, 'doing our own thing' goes straight against the virtue of hope. In fact, it is the door to hopelessness.

So cheer up! Truly cheer up, my dear friends. God is love—and with Him, every moment is the moment of beginning again, and that means every moment is the moment of joy and of hope.

Where Love Is, God Is

Where was Christ born? In a quiet, dry cave, of which there are so many in the Holy Land, and which probably was close to an inn. That is where God was born.

Many miracles attended His birth, but eventually, in utter simplicity and humility, wrapped in the cloak of His mother, who was sitting on a donkey and followed by St. Joseph, Jesus made the slow journey back to Nazareth, back to the home they had left, after being registered at the bidding of a nation that then ruled the world.

Many years later, the Child who had been born in a cave went about doing good and preaching what He called the Good News—that the kingdom was at hand, and that to become a member of this kingdom all a person had to do was to love God, and to love his neighbor as himself. He who is Love wanted all men to know they belonged to God, the God born in a cave.

He went on to speak of loving enemies, and of the greatest love of all—to lay down one's life for a friend. The message was simple. St. Paul, one of His apostles, has said:

> If your life in Christ means anything to you, if love can persuade at all or the Spirit that we have in common, or any tenderness or sympathy, then be united in your conviction and *united in your love*, in a common purpose and a common mind. This is the one thing that would make me completely happy.
>
> There must be no competition among you, no conceit; everybody is to be self-effacing. Always consid-

er everybody better than yourself, so that no one thinks of his own interests first, but everybody thinks of other people's interests instead. (Phil. 2:1–4)

Christmas is with us again. The words of Christ are clear. So are the words of St. Paul.

May your Christmas be full of love for one another. Then it will be merry.

Christmas and Healing

There is a paradox of the divine being in a cradle. Now just stop and think about it. The divine being in a cradle! Everything in us feels joy at this sentence, especially if we have a wrong image of ourselves. It should dissolve, disappear, because when God becomes a Child, then the wrong image of ourselves vanishes. Because in a cradle, in a crib, we see Love so small that we can pick it up. And we look at that cradle and we ask ourselves, why do I think that God does not love me? Here He is. How stupid of me! And slowly, before a crib, this image that most people have of themselves dissolves, and the real person comes out. That is one of the healing processes of God—to draw us to a crib. By so doing, He heals us. We can't refuse the healing.

Think of Christ not only little and in a crib, but poor, and born in a cave. He wanted to be born among the poor. It seems that Christ had a passionate desire to be among the poor from His childhood on, and probably before. That brings us tremendous hope. That should be the second healing of His birth, because who of us isn't poor?

A tremendous healing power comes from the fact that He was in a crib and in a cave. It heals us of this terrible, hopeless, incredible, devilish, senseless, idiotic image that we have of ourselves, that somebody has given us, God rest their souls and have mercy on them. We don't have to keep it, this wrong image of ourselves.

Think too, of Christ depending on a mother as if He were just you and me; now there is a third healing power. Think of that, and how is it possible to have a wrong image of yourself? Just tell me! Because in these situations—God descending into a manger or crib, God being born poor in a cave, and being dependent on a human being—His immense love just about envelopes us, until intellectually, we surrender to that love. It is palpable, it is evident, His love.

Why do we have wrong self-images when God does all those things for us? What do you think about that?

Christ also said, "Unless you love your neighbor whom you can see, there is no possibility of your loving Me, whom you cannot see." So he had two little answers for us: Don't worry about your sins, and, Love your neighbor and you will see Me. That is exactly it.

Think for a minute about the Magi. They were following the star and searching, seeking something new, and even finding something unexpected. That sense of searching still tingles in the Christmas story and in every Christmas celebration, as does the sense of discovery.

So you see, Advent is a time of search, and a time of discovery, and among other things, that search is another gift from God to you and me, because in searching we discover that we cannot have a wrong idea of ourselves. We must love ourselves and accept ourselves. That is the fourth way of healing that is given to us in Advent.

Advent is a good time to think that if I really become a child so that I can sit by the crib and play with God easily, if I really accept myself as God created me, if I allow this fantastic situation to become a reality in me, and if I look at the Child and see myself and lose the wrong image of myself, then evil cannot touch me. In a word, if I have the faith, love and hope that the Child brings as He lays in the manger, then I am immune. Let us pray this Advent for an increase in faith, love and hope.

Looking Into The Child's Eyes

One Christmas, I wrote on my cards, "Give me the heart of a child, *and* the awesome courage to live it out." For an adult, it takes courage to have the trust of a child. You have to be awfully mature to be the kind of child that God wants you to be. At Christmas, we can look into the eyes of the Divine Child, as He lies in the straw, and meditate on this quality of childlikeness.

Small was the cave. Small and graceful was the young mother. Smaller still, against cave and people and animals, was the Baby. And yet, immensity, eternity—*all* the power and glory of God!—were contained in His smallness.

Hidden was the cave. Just a stable that hundreds passed on that holy night, without a glance. Hidden was Mary's most holy secret for nine long months. Hidden was the birth of the Child, hidden from all eyes but Mary's and Joseph's.

Christmas is the feast of littleness and hiddenness. It is the feast of humility, which is the backdrop for the immense, all-consuming flame of charity, of love.

Charity, humility—how our times hunger for them! And how little they know *what* they hunger for! Who, these days, realizes that the peace and happiness which they so vainly seek can be found in those two short words: charity and humility?

The sin of our century is, in truth, against the First Commandment. We have deserted the true God. We have made for ourselves a thousand idols. And then we have merged them all into one, which is covered and represented by the pronoun 'I'. We are worshipers of 'self'. And all our world of gadgets and comforts, of goals and ambitions and achievements, is centered around that idol of 'I'.

Self-centeredness, like a poison, creeps into our waking and sleeping hours. It brings pain and bitterness into our days, and a thousand fears into our dreams. Our self-centeredness becomes pride, which then sets us into the rat race of 'keeping up with the Joneses'.

Our very insecurity demands that we possess more, that we have more—ever bigger and better bank accounts, ever bigger and better and faster cars, more leisure time, and a growing boredom with it!

Because of self-centeredness, the whole world is puffed up, yet insecure. Frightened and insecure, we retreat into unreality. We are shepherded by the very monster we have enthroned as the god and king of our lives—our 'self'!

Needing more and more food for this insatiable 'self', we get lost in a woods conjured up by our imagination. Lost souls. Lost generations. Lost nations. A lost world. All are imprisoned in the 'I' of self-worship. Yet there, right before us!—stands, against the mist of centuries, the first Christmas!

Small was the cave. Small and graceful the young mother. Small, against the cave, people and animals, was the Baby. Yet, immensity, eternity, and all power and glory were contained in His smallness!

Let this Christmas be for us a turning point. Let us kill 'self'. Let us become small enough to kneel at the crib, and big enough just to reach the level of the Baby's eyes. Let us then *look into them*—and catch sight of Love Incarnate! Then we shall be made whole again, and our hunger will be filled.

"For unless you become as a little child, you shall not enter the Kingdom of Heaven."

Journeying with Mary to Bethlehem

Again this Christmas, our spiritual eyes turn toward the old, yet ever new, story of Bethlehem with its stable, manger, mother, Child, St. Joseph, shepherds, and foreign kings.

During Advent, we think about Mary. It is the immensity of God's love and mercy, its infinite depths, that has brought Mary to us sinners. Through her has come to us her Son, who is the Truth and the Way. And this miracle took place in a minor out-of-the-way village called Bethlehem.

In this holy season, let us journey with Mary toward that village. We make this pilgrimage with hearts cleansed by the tears of compunction, with souls filled by humility and simplicity. These are the fruits of our love for the Infant Christ.

As we move closer and closer to the place of the Sacred Birth, the sublime mystery of the Incarnation will open itself before us (at least a little more than now, when we often render but lip service to this mystery). It will enfold us into its glory, and will bring us the peace and joy that we so hunger for.

O Mother most pure, make us pure of heart! May we, this Advent, travel with you along the dusty roads to Bethlehem. May we, this holy Christmas, see Christ as you saw Him, lying on that harsh straw in the stable of Bethlehem.

Being In Tune with God

I look at you today, and I see you as musical instruments. You are perfectly attuned to the will of God, and are becoming a beautiful symphony! Your music penetrates places in this world where the only other sounds seem to be the voices of angry, frightened people who do not know God, and couldn't care less about Him.

I see you as minstrels, learning to sing lullabies to Christ the Child. And I think of you as individual notes in this beautiful melody of the Holy Spirit. I listen to these notes, one by one, and I hope and pray that each one will remain clear and true. The notes of your songs are your daily work, and your attitudes toward life. I pray that no sour notes ever enter your songs to the Christ Child.

I see you attuned to the Holy Spirit, the Great Wind, the ineffable Composer of the songs that the Holy Child likes to hear. I see you cherished by His mother, who waits for you to come and share not only her Christmas joy in the stable of Bethlehem, but her *whole* life, so hidden and wonderful.

It is she who has called us to imitate the lives of the Holy Family in Nazareth. Theirs was a humble and hidden life, composed of ordinary little things, but—oh, how well done, and with great love!

Advent

Is Advent a time of waiting?
A time of learning to sing lullabies?

But where to go, and to whom
To learn to sing songs to God—a Child!

Is then Advent also a time of walking,
On pilgrimage, to learn
How to sing songs to the Holy Child?

Or is it still-time? Faith-time?
Spent awaiting some holy minstrel
To come my way?

Lo, what is this?
Who is knocking
In the dark night upon my door?
Oh! It is only a tree branch
Heavy with newly fallen snow!

The hour is late, and I am sleepy.
But the wind is high, the knocking louder.
I better go, to shake the branch
Loose of its heavy load of snow!

Oh! Night of wonder!
The wind is singing a melody of peace and joy,
Its harps are trees, snow-laden
And tender bushes changed by cold
Into a million bells
That keep ringing lullabies the wind composed
to Christ the Child.

Awake my soul! And listen!
The Mother sent her Spouse
To teach you this Advent
All the Christmas songs
You wanted so ardently
To sing to her own Son!

Childlike Hearts—Mangers for Christ

Christ desires to be born in the manger of our hearts. Are the
doors of our hearts wide open to receive the shepherds, the
Magi, the stray visitors—in a word, humanity? Are they open

to receive every person as Christ would receive each one of us? Are they open to receive those around us in our daily life?

Or do we think it enough to make a manger of our hearts so that we might hold Christ unto ourselves exclusively? If so, that was not what He was born for, and He might bypass the manger of our hearts.

Christ told us that, unless we become like a child, we would not enter the kingdom of heaven. We tend to associate children and Christmas in a very sentimental fashion: a new-born baby is 'cute'; children are 'lovable' creatures. So they are, but that is not what Christ meant. I think He wanted us to have the *heart* of a child.

What does it mean to have the heart of a child? A child is utterly trusting. A child is totally open, uninhibited, simple, direct, and unafraid. A child believes without reservation.

Every morning, after Communion, I go to pray to the Infant of Prague. I say: "Give me the heart of a child. Give me the awesome courage to live what it demands." That's what Christmas means to me, too.

I pray that this coming New Year will be a year in which we will empty our inner 'self' so as to carry the Christ Child comfortably and warmly in our heart. You know, the Child will be comfortable and warm *only* if we love and trust one another.

Here is part of a poem I wrote for you. Think of it as the Christ Child speaking to your heart:

I sought a woman's womb to become Man.
Now I seek a soul to bring My Love to men!
A soul—to be My stable, My manger,
My Bethlehem!

So I take thy poverty into My descending
And fill it to the brim.
Have faith. Have love.
Let My winds and waters fill you up.

You will return and find Me
Within your soul and heart,
Simple and humble—a Child.

The Gurgle of a Baby

Listen! Do you hear the gurgle of a baby? A baby's coo? Almost none of us can resist the gurgle-song of a baby, or a baby's smile. Yes, listen!

It is *His* gurgle! He is in the manger, and He is happy to have become a human being. Consider the incredible nature of what happened. God entered the womb of a human being! God stayed there as every child stays—for nine months. And then He was born! That, my friends, my dearly beloved ones, is the Incarnation.

And God was *happy* to be incarnated because He loves us. Hence, that funny little gurgle is the song of Love, the smile of Love.

Come, let us arise and go together to Bethlehem. We shall all be one around His crib. Seemingly, we are divided by time and space. But when we love, neither time nor space matters. So we shall all be *together* and we shall behold His gurgle, His song, His smile.

Let us remember it forever!—until we meet Him, face to face. His gurgling smile will assuage our depressions, our anxieties, our tensions. And from His smile we will learn to smile and to sing, no matter where we are or what we have to do, because we shall know that our life is one eternal pilgrimage to Bethlehem.

A Modern Bethlehem

The world is a Bethlehem where all the inns have no room for Him. The canyons of modern cities are caveless; the skyscrapers have locked up their entrances. The music of the donkey's hoofs is lost in the swoosh of our endless traffic.

Where, then, shall the Woman give birth to the Wonderful One, in this caveless world, in the Bethlehem with inns that have no room for Him?

Stop the noise of the traffic! Pause in your goalless rush! Stop, you 'organization man', so drunk with the pride of technological madness that it makes you a slave of machines!

See your skyscrapers tremble and dissolve in an avalanche of tears before the voice of the Father. He can make the world a 'cave' that will hold your broken mechanical dreams. He can smash your silly idols, your spaceships, your robots, your homes, as if they are fragile fruits of a potter's wheel.

Stop your noise and listen! Listen to the music of the donkey's hoofs, bearing the weight of the Woman whose hour has come.

Hasten! Make warm the caves of your souls so that the Holy Anointed One may be born in them—or read the writing of destruction on the eternal walls.

Is Your Heart Ready for Christmas?

What kind of birthplace are you providing for the Christ Child? Is the straw shiny and golden and clean? Is the manger solid, and will it hold up under His weight? Are the animals quiet, scrubbed, brushed?

Have you made the door to the stable of your heart secure against the cold winds of apathy, selfishness, indifference, so that these cannot penetrate? Is the dry wood of your sacrifices, your penances, your prayers, ready to be lit to provide warmth in that cold stable?

Are you ready for the coming of Love? Behold, He comes in the womb of a woman! You will catch your first glimpse of Love on the straw of a stable. There He is, emptying Himself, the Lord of Hosts becoming—out of love for us—a Child.

This Child who lies in the manger possesses all power and glory! He has dominion over life and death. Nothing escapes His care. He made all the laws which brought the universe into existence. They were created by Him and are subject to Him. It is the same Child, the same humble Carpenter of Nazareth, the same Man who died naked on a cross, who possesses all power and glory.

Silent Night—Holy Night

The priest spoke.
The Church was dark.
He asked me what I had to tell
On the eve of this holy night?

I was silent
As one stricken dumb,
For I did not know
Where I was nor how I got there.

All I knew was
That Light filled the Church

and my heart.
That I was far away
Somewhere amidst stars
On a swing
Playing with Mother and Child.

And I knew that
Angels were singing.
Or was it the wind?

All I knew
Was that I was free
And eternally young.

Christmas Eve

Waiting for a new life to begin is a most peculiar waiting. There is a certain quality about it, hushed and holy, as if one were in a church. The waiting is both hard and sweet.

I have been a nurse and I have delivered 48 babies, 22 of them without a doctor. And—every time!—the miracle of birth, the miracle of holding the newborn child brought me mentally to my knees and to Bethlehem.

There is nothing more beautiful, I think, than a new-born child. Ah, but when this newborn child is *God*, that is something else again!

Is there any human being who does not respond to the cry of a child? Did you ever consider the first cry of the Child Jesus? That was His first message of love to us. When we know that we are poor, we can easily enter Bethlehem and *answer* that cry.

The waiting of Advent is almost over. We wait for the coming of God.—He's coming! He's coming!—Stretch out your hands and receive the Child.

Christmas is a very special time. I put the Child in your arms, and I ask you to care for Him as if He were your very own baby. Turn to Our Lady and she will teach you how to care for Him.

O Night of Holy Splendor!

This is a night of splendor,
A night of expectancy and joy all tender.

There is in it the scent
Of a thousand opening flowers
And of spring.

How strange, for snow and ice
Still hold the earth imprisoned.

How strange; in the forests
Trees are still asleep.
Nowhere can be seen
The smallest green bud.

This is a night of splendor
With music in the air.

How strange, for beneath
The soft light of a moon, all is
Quiet, white-quilted with snow.

This is a night of splendor,
For somewhere (it seems) a lily
Regal, slim, is shedding its perfume.

How strange, for it is winter.
Lilies do not bloom in the snow.

It is a night of Holy Splendor,
Filled with the sound of a donkey's hoofs
That walk with a strange, joyful cadence
That speaks of Glory Hidden
And other awesome things.

This is a night of Majestic Splendor,
A night of expectancy and joy all tender.

Why is it, then, that my heart
Wonders if it is ready
To be a cradle for a Child?

The Angels Sing Alleluia

Behold! The world is filled with angels' wings and their songs! I am sure you can hear the quiet, slow steps of shepherds coming down from their hills, to see this wondrous event.

The bells of the donkey are muted, because she who traveled on it has arrived! Mary has arrived to that incredible, fantastic, strange place where God chose to be born! The cave, the stable, the manger, call it what you will; it was, above all else, *poor!*

All these wondrous things can be heard and seen by a heart that has purified itself of dross—a heart that has moved up, on God's bidding, higher and higher and ever higher. That is what the Lord does to a soul. He calls out, saying, "Friend, come higher!" I think that you, who are all friends of God, have heard that call. You are ones whose hearts are pure or are being purified by God.

But I must repeat again, for it is so important: God was born in a stable, a manger, a cave. This all adds up to one thing: *He WANTED to be poor at birth*. He came into the world stark naked, as every child born of woman comes forth from the womb. And what is more important, perhaps, He died naked out of love for us.

So the cross and the crib—both made of wood—are of one pattern. The crib begins the pattern, and, somehow, it becomes the cross. It is all as simple as that, beloved.

God loved poverty unto *nakedness*. This means that He made a total surrender, a total commitment to love. It had to be this way, if it were ever to lead to His Resurrection and to ours. Don't you think so?

Christ, who had nowhere to lay His head, said that if we want to follow Him we must be willing to risk everything—relatives, friends, our goods, our life—and to become 'naked' in a sense, to follow His nakedness of soul. So, this Christmas, I give you Christ's poverty. And gently I remind you that His poverty wasn't for poverty's sake but for love's sake.

Take this poverty, this love, into your hands. Put it in your heart. Let it lie there where God can bless it, and transform it, and make it a part of you who are in love with Him! Yes, take this poverty and love, and make it your own; then pass it on to others. You know as well as I do that, in God, poverty is wealth. You know that love is the 'key' to entering the kingdom of human hearts, and God's heart.

If you take this poverty and love, you will become a child. Not childish, but childlike. As a child, you will be able to come very close to the Child in the manger. You won't have to bend too low. No! As a child, you will be able to play with Him and, in playing, learn so much.

Yes, let us take this poverty and love; let us go together to Bethlehem. Let us gather around His crib, and listen to the angels singing: Alleluia! Alleluia! Alleluia!

Christmas

I saw a Child stand,
Royally bedecked
In crown, scepter,
And finely wrought white garments,
And a crimson cloak.
I saw a Child.
And suddenly I knew
The secret of all mystery,
And of all immensity!

Eternity opened
Its sublimity to me.
I looked into
The Face of Ecstasy.
For hidden there
Before my eyes
Was Love
Become a Child
For love of me!

I knelt
Before His smallness,
And knew
I grew.

There before me
Stood the Infant,
Aged a year or two.
And kneeling made me
As small as He.

Child, Man, and Host!
The secret of all mystery
Began with the Infant,
Grew with the Man,
And reached the infinity
Of sublimity
In the smallest of
All things sublime —
A Host!

I saw a Child
And He gave me the key
That opens the Heart
Of Him-Who-Is;
Whom I can please
If I repeat the Child's way:
Grow small,
Quite small.

Then I will be so very big
That I will reach
My Father's hand
And understand
What it means to be
Absorbed
And hidden
In the Lord of Hosts,
A host myself.

Annihilated
Unto death to self;
A piece of bread
To be eaten up
With zeal and love
For Him —
The Child.

Being Christ-Centered

Throughout this beautiful season, I am praying for you. I pray that the Infant may touch your heart and mind and soul with His tiny hands. I pray that He may open you to His own beauty, and to realize that He *needs* you in His Mystical Body!

I pray that you might begin to be Christ-centered, not self-centered. Yes, this is my prayer for you—that you become Christ-centered, Love-centered! It is tragic to behold a world that 'makes Christ wait' to receive our love. It is even more tragic to behold dedicated Christians—those especially chosen by His love—making Him wait.

But when all is said and done, I must come back to this one sentence of John the Beloved: "Little children, let us *love* one another."

I have nothing else to say, really; Love is the very essence of our religion, our faith.

Book II

Customs
&
Feasts

Celebrating the many feast days that mark the Advent and Christmas season, with customs participated in by the entire family, brings home their real meaning as well as that of this holy season.

The following have been part of the Madonna House celebrations for many years. They come from multiple sources as well as from Catherine, and have been modified over the years. You may wish to further adapt them for your family.

The Advent Wreath

The first thing to begin Advent with is the Advent Wreath. It can be made of any kind of greenery found in your part of the world. Traditionally, it is made of evergreens, which represent everlasting life. Its circular shape, without beginning or end, represents eternity. Use your ingenuity to create the base for the greens.

On the circle of greens are fastened four candles, which represent the four Sundays of Advent. Three of the candles should be purple and one pink or rose-colored. The purple stands for a spirit of penance and prayer during the season. The rose candle is for the third Sunday of Advent, sometimes called Rose Sunday or *Gaudete* Sunday. *Guadete* is Latin for 'rejoice,' and is taken from a Mass reading on that Sunday: "Rejoice in the Lord always!"

The Advent Wreath should be displayed in a prominent place and lit daily when the family is together, perhaps before dinner.

The first candle is lit during the first week of Advent by the youngest able member of the family. The second week's candle is lit by the oldest child. The mother of the family lights it the third week, and the father of the family the fourth.

Catherine recalled that, "When I was a little girl growing up in Russia, while the candles on our Advent wreath were lit, my father would slowly and reverently read the epistle and Gospel of the day. He wove the old and the new, the end and the beginning, the Old Law and the New, into a chain of meditations and prayers that would hold all of us together for the rest of our mortal lives. One candle burned on our Advent wreath the first week of Advent. Another was lit as each week passed, until all four were glowing!"

Blessing the Advent Wreath

Before the first candle is lit, the wreath may be blessed:

Leader: The people who have walked in darkness have seen a great light.

All: Upon those who dwelt in the land of gloom, a light has shone.

Leader: Let us pray. Father of creation and Lord of light, bless our Advent wreath [sprinkles it with holy water] and grace us with Your presence as we celebrate the holy season of Advent. May these candles and our lives reflect the light of Christ, who is the Light of the World. He reigns with You and the Holy Spirit forever and ever.

All: Amen.

Each day when the candles are lit, a portion of the Scripture readings from the Mass of the day may be read, a song sung, or spontaneous or memorized prayers offered. The last seven days before Christmas, the 'O' Antiphons may be said or sung.

December 6
Feast of St. Nicholas

Catherine tells the story.

Everyone knows about St. Nicholas, of course, for wasn't he commissioned by the Christ Child Himself (and His darling mother and His good foster father) to come down to earth every Christmas, until the end of time, to tell the children of all the world the story of the Holy Night?

He also comes to bring them gifts from these Holy Three—gifts of faith, hope, and charity—and such other gifts as they in their littleness and simplicity desire, and have asked of the Holy Baby.

It is a good idea to acquaint yourself with the life of this famous saint and with his place at the side of Christ as the Giver of Gifts.

Nicholas was born to devout Christian parents in the fourth century in the country of Myra, in what is now Turkey. He was still a young man when he was made bishop of Lycia, the capital city and a major port. He was a much beloved bishop and became known as 'the father of the poor' because of his care for the 'little ones'.

Nicholas is greatly honored in the East. And we in the West are indebted to our sisters and brothers in the faith in Russia, Turkey, Greece, the Middle East and Holland for the many stories and legends that have been preserved about him.

There is the story of the time when he heard of a father who was contemplating selling his daughters into prostitution because there was no food left in the house. Nicholas got three sacks of gold coins together and, under the cover of night, threw them into an open window of the house, to be used as a dowry for the girls.

Another time, sailors were about to capsize in their boat on the stormy Aegean Sea. So they called to Holy Nicholas, and the boat came to shore safely with all its passengers and cargo intact.

There are many legends of his protection and help being given to others. Because of this, St. Nicholas has become known as the patron of sailors, and especially of young people and children.

In the Netherlands, children leave their shoes outside on the eve of his feast, knowing that St. Nicholas will fill them with small candies—provided, of course, that they've been good. Children in other countries leave their stockings out for him to fill, rather than shoes.

'Santa Claus' is the Dutch version of this saint's name. *Santa Nikolaus.* Because of his famous visits to the Netherlands in past centuries, he is known to appear in this century at a great number of Christmas parties in North America. Whenever we hear of his presence, it is well to remember that he is really there as a messenger of the Little Infant. The Christ Child, being too small at the moment, cannot deliver Christmas presents Himself. So He has commissioned St. Nicholas, now shortened to 'Santa Claus', to do it in His stead.

When I was a little girl in Russia, what we called 'Saint Nick' was a mammoth gingerbread, all decked out in pink, green, and white icing. Sometimes he was as big as a real baby! Only one Saint Nick was baked in any household, and you had to be very good all through the year to get a Saint Nick to eat. You worked hard for him all through the year. Oh yes, you certainly did! You had to be the *best* child in the family, the most deserving, to get a Saint Nick.

My favorite was made in the shape of a Child in swaddling clothes.

At Madonna House, the kitchen crew bakes a gingerbread man for each person, and a bigger, decorated St. Nicholas gingerbread bishop for each table. The tables are festive that day, with a few little trimmings.

After the evening meal, a special visitor is announced: a member dressed as St. Nicholas in bishop's garb walks through the dining room to deliver a special kind of gift.

In a basket he carries are the names of each person present, printed on small decorative cards. Each person draws a card from the basket (making sure not to get his or her own name!) and thus receives the gift of someone special for whom to pray during the rest of the year.

December 8
Feast of the Immaculate Conception

Catherine writes:

To commemorate this blessed occasion, we can make it a festive day. The food can be extra-special, something more than the ordinary fare. A special cake can be baked, for Our Lady. It can be 'presented' to her, before some picture or statue of the Virgin, before it is shared with the family as dessert. Perhaps a suitable Marian hymn can be sung.

Why do we honor the Virgin Mary? Because she is the Mother of God. It is good to remember that she was, through a unique favor from God, completely without sin from the moment of her conception, in order that she might be 'worthy' to become the Mother of the Son of God. Hence, we call this day the feast of her Immaculate Conception.

December 12
Feast of Our Lady of Guadalupe

There is a great devotion, especially among Mexicans, to Our Lady of Guadalupe. She is the Queen of the Americas, and the patroness of the Mexican people.

This feast day commemorates the appearance of the Blessed Virgin in 1531 to Juan Diego, a poor Indian, on Tepeyac hill, outside what is now Mexico City. Mary asked him to go to the bishop to request that a church be built in her honor, but the bishop did not believe Juan—until Our Lady provided him with fresh roses, growing in the midst of winter.

Juan filled his cloak with the roses, and when he opened it before the bishop, his cloak was found to have a miraculous imprint of Our Lady on it. She was dressed as an Indian princess, surrounded by symbols of the Indian culture.

In a few short years thousands of Indians pilgrimed to the image, and were converted to Christianity. The cloak with Our Lady's image is still intact today, displayed in her cathedral in Mexico City.

The feast of Our Lady of Guadalupe is perhaps the most childlike celebration of the entire year at Madonna House. This whole day is filled with reverence and gratitude for Our Lady, the Mother of God, and with childlike fun.

The day begins with a daybreak serenade of the women by the men, singing in Spanish, with guitar accompaniment. Spanish songs and hymns give the Mass that day a festive flavor, as does the Mexican food for supper, which is usually some combination of tortillas, beans and rice. After supper, some of the community present a dramatization of the story of Our Lady of Guadalupe.

Then everyone improvises a Mexican costume to wear for our 'piñata' party. In recent years we've made papier-mâché piñatas in the form of animals (e.g. an elephant or donkey), and filled them with candies and nuts. The piñata is then hung from the ceiling of the room, and a person is blindfolded. This person attempts to find the piñata and break it with a hammer or bat. As soon as the piñata is broken, the candies and other treats fall onto the floor and there is a mad scramble for them!

We end the evening by gathering around an image of Our Lady and singing a hymn to her.

December 13
Feast of St. Lucy

On St. Lucy's feast day, we have the Hungarian custom of planting a handful of wheat seeds. The wheat represents Christ.

This is an easy custom for anyone to do. Use a wide flower pot or container of earth and plant the wheat evenly over the whole surface. Keep it in a warm room and water it daily. The person who waters the wheat says this little prayer: "All ye things that spring up in the earth, bless the Lord!"

At Christmas, this pot of beautiful new green wheat is placed at the foot of the crib which, of course, is the centerpiece and center of our life during Christmastide. It stands underneath the Christmas tree until Epiphany.

St. Lucy's day comes in Advent because her name ties her with Christ, the Light that comes at Christmas, the Orient from on High, to light those who dwell in darkness. Because of this, she is the patroness of the blind and hers is the Feast of Light in many countries, such as Sweden. In fact the name Lucia, or Lucy, means 'light'. Her feast falls near the shortest day of the year, to remind us that although the daylight may be short, the Light of the World, Christ, is soon coming into the world.

We observe the Swedish custom of making a crown of some solid cardboard into which small candles are placed. One of the younger women is suitably costumed as the virgin martyr St. Lucy, wearing a long, white dress. She makes her appearance in the dining room, which is darkened. Her crown of candles glows in the darkness, representing the Light of Christ!

The costumed St. Lucy walks throughout the room, and from her lighted crown of candles a candle on each table is lit. In past years, we have made little cupcakes, each with a cake candle in it, and one person from each table lit his or her cupcake candle from St. Lucy's candle crown, then passed the light on to the rest at the table—thus passing the light of Christ to everyone in the house.

This little custom is another way of teaching that Christ is the Light of the world, come to light our darkened world.

December 17–23
The 'O' Antiphons

The seven holy days before Christmas are filled with the songs of the beautiful 'O' Antiphons. These are part of Vespers, the Church's evening prayers. They are magnificent petitions, calling on God to come and dwell with us. Their unusual title is based on the fact that each Antiphon begins with the letter 'O' and then calls on God for help under one of His titles. Each Antiphon contains the cry "Come"! They are a tremendous preparation for Christmas. Let us look a little closer at the Antiphons, one by one.

The meditations are by Catherine.

December 17—O WISDOM, *all-holy Word of God, You came forth from the mouth of the Most High, and govern all creation with Your strong yet tender care. COME and teach us Your way of prudence!* (Cf. Wisd. 8:1 and Sir. 24:1–5)

Divine Wisdom comes out of God's mouth, the Wisdom that "in the beginning" created all things. God continues down the centuries to speak to each generation, through the marvels of creation and through His revelation of the ancient Testament. And now He sends us the Christ, the Word of God, the Word that is to teach us the way to God Himself!

We beg the Lord, "Come, and teach us Your way of prudence." What kind of prudence do you think He is going to teach us? Certainly not *human* prudence, which is but a composite of timidity, shyness, fear, and oftentimes avarice. Oh, no! But what, then, *is* God's prudence?

When we first hear of it, it sounds like utter foolishness. Whoever tries to save his life in this world, shall lose it; whoever is willing to risk losing his life—for God's sake!—will end up by saving it. (Cf. Matthew 10:39.)

It is the folly of the Beatitudes. And when all is said and done, it is the folly of the Two Commandments of Love, for truly, if I am to love my neighbor as myself, then I must die to myself. And dying to self is folly to human eyes, as is the idea of loving your enemies.

If we read the Bible 'on our knees' as it were, with our eyes and ears open, and with our heart, soul, and mind attuned to the sacred words, we will begin to understand this Divine Prudence of which the Antiphon speaks. This will not be hard, for the examples of God's Prudence and Wisdom are endless.

December 18—O ADONAI, *God of the Covenant, and King of Israel, You appeared to Moses in the flame of the burning bush, and You gave him the sacred law on Mount Sinai. COME now! With an outstretched arm, redeem us!* (Cf. Exod. 3:2–10 and 20:1–21)

Christ, the Lord, who is God Most High and Son of God, was at work with the Father during the early days of Israel, in the time of the First Covenant. He comes to us now, establishing a New Covenant in our hearts, with the task of delivering us from the power of Satan and bringing us into His kingdom.

To Moses, God appeared in a flaming bush in the desert and as thunder and lightning on the mountain. To us, He appears in a humble piece of bread—the Eucharist. Do we *realize* the fire and flame that comes to us?

We are called to accept this fire and flame into our being, so that we can go forth and, in every step of ours, shed this flame, this fire of love, upon all the earth so that it may be renewed. For that is the desire of Christ the Lord!

For *this* He came: to restore His kingdom to His Father. *We* are that kingdom, and He bade us to continue its restoration by going to the very limits of the earth to preach His New Covenant, His Gospel of love, and to spread the fire and flame of the Holy Spirit.

How do we preach that Gospel? We cry it with our *lives!* Yes, you and I must 'cry the Gospel' with our very being! We can do this through little things, such very little things, if they are done well, and with a great love of God. We know that, even in 'little things' we are truly *restoring* the world to Christ.

And as we do this, Christ will show us the needs of our brothers and sisters, our friends and neighbors. He will give us the grace to fill those needs, one by one, as they arise before our eyes. This restoration will not be done in any spectacular fashion, but in a humble, quiet way. In this manner, we will be doing what St. John the Beloved told us to do: *Little children, love one another!* (Cf. 1 John 3:11-18.)

This 'O' Antiphon brings this passage to my mind so vividly! I hope and pray that my words may contain for you a spark of that fire that appeared in a burning bush to Moses, so that you may catch fire and become yourself a burning bush before the Lord!

December 19—O ROOT OF JESSE, *Your flowering stem has been raised up as a sign to all the nations. Before You, kings shall be struck silent, and faraway peoples shall come to adore and beg mercy. COME and deliver us. Do not delay!* (Cf. Isa. 11:1 and 11:10 and 52:15)

Christ, in his humanity, is the descendant of Jesse (the father of David in the Old Testament). He comes to establish the universal kingdom of God. And we cry out to Him: *Come! Please! Hurry! Do not delay!*

This should be the prayer of every moment. It goes hand in hand with that prayer of the heart that was prayed by the Russian pilgrim: "Lord Jesus Christ, have mercy on me a sinner." How easily the cry of this Antiphon fits in with that prayer of the heart!

We need to be delivered. Delivered from our emotions that impede our way to God. Delivered from our doubts that act like cold water on the fire of the Holy Spirit. Delivered from our sins, even if they are as small as a grain of sand, for a grain of sand can stop huge machinery should it enter the vital part.

We need to be delivered from Satan and his hordes, who forever roam around about us "like a roaring lion" seeking whom they may devour. (Cf. 1 Pet. 5:8.)

Yes, this Antiphon is a fitting prayer to say as our longings and our desires and our need for Him increases. For it ends with the ringing words: *Come! Come and deliver us! Do not delay!!*

December 20—O KEY OF DAVID *and Ruler of the House of Israel, You have the power to open the gates of kingdoms, and no one can resist it. COME and liberate the captives from their prison-house, and lead them into freedom.* (Cf. Isa. 22:22 and Rev. 3:7 and Matt. 16:18–19.)

Christ comes to save us, to liberate us from sin. We are all prisoners of sin and yet we all have the key to our prison, and to that of others. That key is love!

Love is the fruit of faith—faith in the Lord Christ, and in the Father, and in the Holy Spirit. Now that the Lord has come and has given us the key, we can enter the prison of our emotions, our doubts, our temptations, our fears, and our perversity.

With faith and love, we open the doors of our own prison. And once we have liberated ourselves from our own prison, we can go forth and set free our neighbors—one by one. We can liberate others from their own prison of doubts, sins, and temptations. We do so by bringing them the Glad Tidings of God's *Immense Love* for them—and by leading them back to God.

As His ministers, we have the keys to our Father's house. And one of the mansions of our Father is the soul of our neighbor.

December 21—O DAWN OF THE EAST,

Radiant Brightness of Light Eternal, and Sun of Justice, COME and enlighten those who dwell in darkness and in the shadow of death. (Cf. Pss. 107, 106:10–16 and Luke 1:78–79.)

Christ is the Truth. He is the One whose very Presence illuminates human life, and He comes to bring the plentitude of revelation. We are apostles of His, especially chosen by Him to extend His light into the world, to bring His truth to men in an age when the Prince of Lies seems to rule over the majority of the world.

Symbolically, we have to enter the mist of Satan. He wants to confuse, to bring mists and fogs of every shade into the world, from light gray to black, and all in between.

He uses fogs and mists to make the day seem like twilight. He prefers the twilight to the night because, when it is totally dark, people stay away from it. But people think they can find their way in fog and so they venture in, and get lost.

In the mist, truth and untruth lose their boundaries. People think they are walking the straight path of the Lord when, in actuality, they may have already ventured onto the wide road of Satan, or into one of his thousand twisted paths.

The Lord has chosen us to light the way into the mist with lamps of our faith and love. We must take plenty of oil for our lamps, like the wise virgins awaiting the Coming of the Bridegroom. (Cf. Matt. 25:3–7.)

With the oil of God's truth, we can sail forth into the mist. It is God's oil and God's light, and wherever the ray of that light reaches, it destroys the mist of Satan. Then we can 'see', because we will be living in the light of God's truth.

This is why we are so important to the Church. Each of our lamps may appear small, but there are many of us. And the light we carry is not ours, but Christ's—and what could be more immense, and more potent, against the mists and fogs of Satan?

December 22—O KING OF THE GENTILES,

the Desired One of the Nations, You are the cornerstone of the Church, uniting all peoples into one. COME and deliver us, whom You have shaped and formed from the dust of the earth. (Cf. Isa. 60:4–11 and Eph. 2:14–22 and Job 10:8–9.)

Christ is the foundation of the new order, in which all distinctions between the Jewish people and the pagan nations are erased. We are no longer to consider ourselves Jew or Gentile, master or slave. In Christ, all prejudice, exclusiveness, separateness is abolished from our hearts, if we will allow it.

Christ is the New Adam, in which the Father sees the achievement of His design for the human race. He comes now to incorporate us into Himself, to graft us onto Himself, and to recapture unto Himself the whole of the universe.

By this incorporation into Christ, we are made members of his Mystical Body. Does the arm wage war on the foot? Or the heart on the liver? Or the eyes on the mouth? Or the mouth on the ear? An arm that is cut off is a dead arm; it doesn't belong to the body anymore. (Cf. 1 Cor. 12:12–30.)

We must harbor no prejudices against those of different races, nationalities or creeds. We must tear out such prejudices by the roots, no matter how deep they are. We will do this the moment we begin to love and serve Christ the Lord, for no one can truly love until the heart is free from all prejudices.

December 23—O EMMANUEL, *our King and Lawgiver, and Savior of all peoples, COME and dwell with us, O Lord our God.* (Cf. Isa. 7:14 and 33:22; Matt. 1:23.)

Christ is God-made-man. He comes to dwell among us. This earth has borne His imprint and we walk on it, each step of ours an adventure in faith, love, and hope.

How can we *not* love this earth upon which He walked? How can we *not* get from it the strength that the imprints of His feet have left there? Because, you know, His footprints are still in its dust, and His blood is still mixed with it.

How can we enter anyplace where the Blessed Sacrament reposes, and *not* be filled with joy, and renewed in hope and in strength? Yes, He has come! He will be coming again in the Parousia, but He is with us *now!* He is Emmanuel ('God with us')—in thousands of Presences, too immense to enumerate.

The earth bears His footprints, and it has drunk of His blood, which fell in the garden and at the flagellation, and at Calvary. The same earth that heard the sound of his voice will, if we ask it, bring back the echo of His voice, and our faith will listen joyously.

Straw will speak to us. Wood will sing to us of Him. For He was born in it, worked in it, died on it. 'Touching wood' in a moment of pain, in a moment of temptation, will give us strength in that same faith.

The stars speak of Him, and the moon and the sun, for they have all beheld His glory on earth, from birth to death! Above all, a piece of bread—which is not a piece of bread, but which is Christ Himself in our tabernacle—is here. It is God-with-us!

Christ multiplies Himself in His priests. And we can find the image of His face in our neighbor. Oh, dearly beloved, how very privileged we are to have all these graces, all these helps, which are given to us so that we become strong in faith, in hope, and in love!

Christmas Decorating

The ingenuity of love can create many beautiful decorations from very little: see also Catherine's story of the First Christmas in Combermere on page 123.

As Catherine said, "For Christmas we decorate!" And at Madonna House, the decorations that grace the buildings inside and out are prepared with love, prayer and patience, in order to make it as beautiful as possible, in an expression of love for God and neighbor.

"Let every guest be received as Christ," reads the sign near the front door, and guests are received with respect and love.

Wreaths are the sign of welcome to the stranger in our midst. They are the sign of the circle of love, established by Christ. They symbolize the eternity of love, to which we are going, and they are the sign of hospitality.

Since evergreens are abundant in Combermere, we use them to make many of these fresh, fragrant wreaths, which family and visitors see when they arrive. As Catherine always emphasized, we put the gift of ourselves into this decoration. It is the most importand gift we can give to each other and to God.

Since the greens keep well, they are made ahead of time, decorated with pine cones and donated Christmas ornaments.

What material is abundant in your area? Use whatever is available, whether it be a holly tree in your yard, dried plants, even a palm tree! Use the trimmings from a Christmas tree lot to decorate: smaller twigs of pine or fir can top a shelf or fill a big bowl. Add a few shiny Christmas balls for an attractive, fragrant centerpiece.

We use ornaments that we've made of woven wheat, along with Christmas balls hung with sewing thread from the ceilings to form mobile-like groupings over the tables. This idea could lend itself to both beauty and practicality in homes where toddlers can see the pretty things, safely out of reach of little hands.

At one end of our dining room is a display of dolls, representing people from all over the world, dressed in their native costumes. It reminds us that we are not alone in our joy. "The glory of the Lord will be revealed, and all mankind together will see it". (Isa. 40:5)

The focal point of our decorations is the crèche, which has a place of special honor beneath the Christmas tree.

The main idea is to express, through decorations, one's love for God and neighbor during this wonderful season.

Baking Christmas Foods

Catherine writes about cooking:

The preparation of food, as well as its acquisition, has always been an expression of love. This act became exceedingly holy with the Coming of Christ. His mother sanctified it in a very special manner by transforming the fruits of the earth for the nourishment of His Human Body, which He assumed for our sake at Christmas-time.

The act of preparing food became even more holy when Christ, the Lord, used bread and wine to feed us, by transforming them into His Body and Blood.

The holiness of the kitchen is beyond the ability of human words to express. To lovingly and joyfully transform the raw products of God's earth into food to feed one's brothers and sisters: this is a service and a privilege almost beyond compare!

Those who work in the kitchen are especially blessed, for they 'feed the hungry' in the most literal of terms. They are blessed, because Our Lord said, "Whatsoever you do to the least of these, you do to Me." Those who eat of this food are also blessed, because they are like the disciples who sat at table with Jesus, in the village inn at Emmaus, "And they knew Him in the breaking of bread."

May the Lord, who used bread and wine to feed us so lovingly with Himself, bless all those who cook and prepare food. May He show them His Face in the faces of all those who sit down to partake of the meals they have so lovingly prepared.

Singing Christmas Carols

Madonna House has a tradition of carolling its neighbors in Combermere, Ontario and the surrounding areas of the countryside. On an appointed evening after supper, a few groups of singers, warmly bundled against the northern Ontario cold, go from house to house and sing a traditional carol or two for each home they visit.

Each group carries a cross, made with two rough branches of a tree, or two planks of wood, and with a tinsel star placed in the middle of it. An old-fashioned kerosene barn-lantern (plus a few flashlights) provide light for the group.

Singing together is a beautiful way to honor the Savior, the Infant of Bethlehem—as well as a good way to meet with friends, family and neighbors. Singing is a personal gift of praise and love; singing together the familiar, beloved carols of Christmas is a beautiful way to give the gift of love to Christ in your neighbors.

Afterwards, the carollers warm up with hot chocolate, tea, or hot cider and a Christmas cookie or two. The carolling can be done before or after Christmas, but sometime during the season.

Christmas carols of different countries are commonly sung in our dining room after meals. Usually French and English carols predominate; but Irish, Polish, Ukrainian, West Indian and Spanish carols also proliferate. The reason for this is that—at Christmas—every land sings, the whole earth sings!

The essence of Christmas is to love one another. And what better way to love our brothers and sisters of the whole earth than to learn songs in their languages to praise God?

Blessing of the Christmas Tree

During the week before Christmas, a tree is put up and decorated. When it is ready it can be blessed before the lights are turned on for the first time. Psalm 95/96 can be recited by a reader (or two readers alternately):

Antiphon: Let all the trees of the forest sing for joy, for the Lord has come.

All repeat antiphon.

O sing a new song to the Lord,
sing to the Lord all the earth.
O sing to the Lord, bless His name.
Proclaim His help day by day,

tell among the nations His glory
and His wonders among all the peoples.

All repeat antiphon.

The Lord is great and worthy of praise,
to be feared above all gods;
the gods of the heathens are naught.

It was the Lord who made the heavens,
His are majesty and state and power
and splendor in His holy place.

All repeat antiphon.

Give the Lord, you families of peoples,
give the Lord glory and power,
give the Lord the glory of His name.

Bring an offering and enter His courts,
worship the Lord in His temple.
O earth, tremble before Him.

All repeat antiphon.

Proclaim to the nations: "God is king."
The world He made firm in its place;
He will judge the peoples in fairness.
Let the heavens rejoice and the earth be glad,
let the sea and all within it thunder praise,
let the land and all it bears rejoice.
All you trees of the forest, shout for joy
at the presence of the Lord for He comes,
He comes to rule the earth.

With justice He will rule the world,
He will judge the peoples with His truth.

All: Glory to the Father, to the Son and to the Holy
Spirit, as it was in the beginning is now and will be
forever. Amen.

All repeat antiphon.

*The symbolism of the tree is then explained, and the tree is
blessed:*

After the fall of our first parents, the earth was bare
and desolate; the world stood in the darkness of sin.
But when the Savior was born, our earth shone with a
new brightness; the glory of the Almighty Father had
renewed the world, making it more beautiful than
before.

This tree once stood dark and empty in a cold
world. But now glowing with lights and ornaments in
its new glory, this Christmas tree reflects the new
beauty God brought to earth when "the Word was
made flesh and dwelt among us." By a tree the whole
world has been redeemed, and therefore, with great
joy we celebrate the glory of this tree.

We beseech you, O Holy God, Father Almighty, to
bless this tree, which we have adorned in honor of the
new birth of your only-begotten Son, and may you
brighten our souls and bodies with the richness and
beauty of your grace. Then inwardly enlightened by
your splendor shining in this tree, may we come like
the wise men to adore Him who is eternal Light and
beauty, the same Jesus Christ, your Son, our Lord.
Amen.

Christmas Eve

The joyous celebration of the birth of Christ begins with the traditional Mass at midnight. The path to the Madonna House chapel is lined with luminaria, or little candles placed in paper or glass containers. Their lights flicker in welcome, reminding us that Christ is the Light of the World, come to earth to light up the darkness.

Just before the liturgy begins, the family observes a Mexican custom called the Posadas. In Mexico, people carry lanterns in procession at night and re-enact the journey to Bethlehem. A couple representing Joseph and Mary knock on the door three times, begging admittance, while those inside respond. After each of the first two knocks, those inside gruffly tell the Holy Family there is no room for them. But after the third knock their hearts change and they welcome the Holy Family. Then all sing: "Enter into our home, holy pilgrims. Come to us with your peace and your love. Bear thy holy Child in our midst, Blessed Mother, for He comes down from heaven above!"

The Mass follows, with many traditional Christmas carols. A joyous three-fold strain, especially for Christmas, is sung at the completion of the Eucharistic Prayer:

Christ is Born! Glorify Him!
Christ has come from heaven! Receive Him!
Christ is now on earth! Oh, be jubilant! . . .

After Mass, a light meal is served. There is much singing and gaiety, conversation and games that continue into the wee hours. Carols from various countries are sung in different languages.

Christmas

A Shepherd's Mass, the second Mass of Christmas, is celebrated in the early hours of the morning. A large, festive holiday dinner is served Christmas evening.

The Twelve Days of Christmas stretch from Christmas Day to January 6th, which is traditionally the celebration of Epiphany. Throughout the dozen days, Christmas songs are sung and Christmas foods are eaten. It is also a time to visit friends and family, and to exchange gifts with them.

December 27
Feast of St. John the Beloved

This beautiful Austrian custom for celebrating this feast is fairly widespread in many parts of Europe. It can easily be adapted to groups or families.

The story is based on ancient legend, rather than the Bible. One version has it that John was challenged to drink a cup of poisoned wine to prove that Christ was truly God. He did so, without ill effect, and converted his onlookers to Christianity. Another version has it that John was surreptitiously handed a poisoned cup to drink. But when he blessed it with the sign of the cross, the cup broke in half, spilling its deadly contents out onto the ground.

Thus, to offer someone The Love of St. John is to give "the perfect love that casts out all fear" (Cf. 1 John 4:18).

At the beginning of the evening meal, a carafe of wine and a platter of bread is blessed. The prayer below has been adapted from *The Roman Ritual*.

Let us pray: If it please You, Most Holy Spirit, come to us to bless this wine and this bread by the power of Your Divine Presence. Grant that, through the prayers of St. John the Beloved, apostle and evangelist, we who taste of this wine and eat of this bread will find it a help and a protection. O Holy Spirit, we offer ourselves to You, body and soul, so that we may be cleansed and purified, healed and strengthened, and made ready for Your Service. Amen.

After the blessing, a small amount of wine is poured into each person's glass. The platter of bread, which has previously been cut in squares of one inch or so, is passed around the table, so that each person can take one piece.

Whoever is at the head of the table then turns to the person on the left, toasts him or her, as well as clinking glasses, holds out a piece of bread, and says in a voice loud enough for everyone to hear, "I give you The Love of St. John."

The other person grasps half of the bread and, as it is broken in two, replies, "I thank you for The Love of St. John." Then the two consume their half of the bread and take a sip of wine.

The second person then takes up a piece of bread and offers it to the person on the left in the same manner, again clinking glasses and saying, "I give you The Love of St. John." The bread is given as before, with the person responding, "I thank you for The Love of St. John."

This is repeated until all at the table have clinked glasses, offered a piece of bread to another, broken it in two, sipped a little wine, and eaten the ceremonial bread.

When this is done, the meal is served. Some of the wine may be served with the dinner. Some can be put into a decanter, and kept for medicinal purposes at other times of the year.

Catherine comments on this feast:

Long ago and far away, an ordinary man called John laid his head on the breast of Christ and listened to the heartbeats of the Lord. Who can venture to guess what that man felt as he heard the beat of that mighty Heart?

None of us can ever be in his place, but all of us could hear—if we would but listen—the heartbeats of God, the song of love that He sings to us, whom He has loved so much.

If we meditated on the Most Holy Sacrament of the Eucharist, we would not only hear His heartbeats, we would hear our own hearts beating in unison with His. We would be united with our Lord and our God.

God's heart is the only true resting place for all of us, the real oasis to which God calls us. But the key to His heart is *identification* with Him and with all those He calls His little ones.

This deep love of humanity requires an enlargement of heart that is so great that we could not aspire to it unless God showed us the way. We must pray for that enlargement of heart. And we must act by 'reaching out'—to touch God with one hand and to touch our fellow man with the other. In this way, we become cruciform.

By doing this, we enter into a new dimension of faith and prayer. And this helps the Lord to enlarge our heart.

December 28
Feast of the Holy Innocents

This feast commemorates the infants who suffered death at the hands of Herod's soldiers who were seeking to kill the child Jesus (cf. Matt. 2:13–18). A feast in their honor has been observed since the fifth century.

This is a special day for parents to bless their children. Simply trace the sign of the cross with holy water on the child's forehead and say, "May God bless you [child's name] in the name of the Father, and of the Son, and of the Holy Spirit." (Many parents give this blessing just before bedtime each day.)

Catherine commented on this feast:

I'd like to share with you my meditations on this day of the Holy Innocents. I was thinking of all those who are being 'murdered' these days, and I am not ashamed to say that I cried.

I cried over all of us. The innocent ones are not only little children (who indeed are innocent, whether babies or children). There are adults, too, who have innocent hearts, and who seek with their innocent hearts the way to God.

I thought of the people who delight in destroying innocence with words. Words are such wonderful things. Words console. Words strengthen. Our words can be like hands stretched out to our brothers and sisters, inviting them to walk the path of God. But our words can be terrible also. They can be hands that tear our brother or sister apart; they can be a voice that calls them seductively down twisted pathways, to all kinds of dark and dank depths.

People use paint remover on chairs. We, so many of us, use something that by 'a single stroke' can tear the innocence out of people's hearts. Quite suddenly, because of our stupid or malicious act, they seem to forget their own childlikeness.

The image of God in a manger disappears from their minds. Darkness and doubt begin to well up inside them. They go on to ridicule the whole idea of Christmas, the whole idea of Incarnation. And they end up by saying that God doesn't exist at all. All because of our words!

How many people, if they go really deep into their hearts, find that they have destroyed the innocence in others? They have been eager to impart evil instead of good.

Gossip is one way of rubbing out that innocence. We believe in somebody, and trust that person. But somebody else (a close 'friend' perhaps) is eager, and for some reason almost happy, to destroy the person in whom we might believe. Why?

There are so many lovely innocent people who, as they walk the countries of the world, can almost hear the baying pack of wolves (male or female) that want to get their fangs into that innocence and tear it apart.

Herod was part of a very small kingdom, and the children he killed were comparatively few. People today do their killing on a big scale. They want to 'convert' people from their silly religious ideas into the plain 'facts of life', into the realities of science and technology. They do not admit that religion and science can co-exist. They desire to take God out of the human heart entirely.

How many of us are guilty of having done this? Have we, at one time or another, said to someone: "Don't tell me you believe in that trash? You mean to say you go to Mass, you say the rosary, you believe in that mythical God? When are you going to 'wise up' about life?" We might not have said these words to others, but we have listened to them. And we have said them to ourselves. Words can influence us so tremendously!

But there is a great miracle in God, a great gift of God: *lost innocence can be restored!* Have we told others about this gift? Have we spoken to our friends, to our enemies, to ourselves about it—we who are supposedly bringing the Good News to the world?

Confession is the way to restore innocence. Once we have repented and have met Christ in this Sacrament, He touches us in our inmost being and we become as innocent as new-born babies.

To the Russians, confession is 'the kiss of Christ'! My mother used to tell me that, although the priest is not Christ, he speaks in the name of Christ. He speaks in such a way that it is Christ who kisses me in confession.

Since we were far away from a Catholic Church, I trotted off to the Orthodox Church for confession. There was this nice bearded man and he sat right in the midst of the big church. (They don't have a little room or corner where you go and talk things out in secret.)

I was about seven years old and I told the priest all about stealing apples from the next-door neighbor's orchard. He forgave me, put me on his lap, and kissed me. I came home jumping from one leg to the other and I walked in waltzing and I said, "Mommy, Christ kissed me—but he has an awfully big beard." For a very long time, I thought Christ had a beard—one of those bushy things that's very difficult to be kissed with.

Even though God can restore innocence through this Sacrament, we go around very sophisticatedly and say to others: "Oh, you go to confession? You know, that is *passé*. It just isn't done anymore." I've heard that over and over again! It's another way of taking away from the innocent the return to their innocence. Have we got the right to do this?

Why don't we stop it? Why not stop the strange, perverse human desire (I think it is begotten by Satan) to spoil the other if we are spoiled, to tear off the shininess of somebody else by finding some fault in them, and then declaring: "Oh, you think that he or she is good? Well, just take a look at this!" Why do we do this? Why do we approach everybody with a critical eye?

All these things came to mind as I thought about this strange feast of Herod's killing. Yes, there are thousands of ways of killing innocence. And there are thousands of ways of stopping it from being restored by Him who was completely innocent.

Let us guard our hearts and our lips this day (and every day), that we may not be guilty of tearing innocence away from anybody. And if it happens that we have done so, let us have compunction and sorrow over it. And, in repentance, let us lead that person to the one place where innocence can be restored—the lips of Our Lord Jesus Christ.

The Feast of the Holy Family

This feast is usually celebrated on the Sunday that comes between Christmas and New Year's Day. It commemorates the Holy Family—Jesus, Mary, and Joseph—as the model of family holiness. The Holy Family was the first 'domestic church' and is a great help to today's modern families who want to become holy.

Now we come back to the question of 'how to preach the Gospel with our lives.' Again, we look to the Holy Family for examples. They lived the Law fully and completely; for Christ came to fulfill the Law not to abolish it. But He gave us a New Law, and it is that New Law that we have to live, just as the Holy Family lived the will of the Father in the Old Law—*without compromise!*

Our poverty should be the poverty of Nazareth, and of the Holy Family. They were artisans. They had enough to live simple and uncomplicated lives. They were not destitute. But their poverty was *luminous* because all three of them were utterly detached from their own wills and completely attached to the will of God the Father. Here an endless wealth of meditation presents itself to all of us.

Nazareth is our model and our spiritual home. Like the Holy Family, we seek to be a community of love, of caritas, of poverty, of detachment from self and self-will. We lead an ordinary life, filled with many monotonous jobs to be done with great love for God and neighbor.

Through these little daily tasks, we become 'witnesses' of God. What does that mean? I would define it as follows: "To be a witness does not consist in engaging in propaganda, or even in stirring people up, but in being *a living mystery*. It means to live in such a way that *one's life would not make sense* if God did not exist."

On another occasion Catherine wrote:

Can you imagine the depths of unity that must exist between a husband and wife who mutually seek to find God *through* one another rather than *in* one another?

God wants their relationship to be a totality of love for Him. And because He loves them so passionately—and because He wants to hand them *Himself* so totally—He keeps calling them to an ever-greater faith, to a higher plateau, to a closer union with Him.

"Bear with one another."(Cf. Col. 3:13) Now, this can be one of the hardest things to do, even in a Christian community, and especially in a close family setting. When St. Francis Xavier was in Spain with the other Jesuits, a couple of his companions said to St. Ignatius: "Take him out of our midst. He is insufferable, because he's *too* holy!"

That's the way it goes with all of us. We 'just barely' can bear with one another. We don't do it with too great an ease, even when everyone is on their best behavior. St. Paul, who was pretty smart about these things, knows what the outcome will be. He continues: "Forgive each other as soon as a quarrel begins. The Lord has forgiven you; now you must do the same." That's rather obvious, isn't it? If the Lord forgives us, we have to turn around and do the same with others.

Let us beg Jesus to know how to love 'without counting the cost'!

December 31—New Year's Eve

At Madonna House, the New Year is welcomed with a Holy Hour of prayer, and silent adoration, and a slow, prayerful reading aloud of the names of all the nations and countries of the world. Catherine gave this talk one New Year's Eve.

At Madonna House, the New Year is not celebrated with a lot of balloons and drinking and carousing. It is celebrated with peace, and joy, and simplicity.

This is the moment of beginning again. It is the threshold between the old and the new. God gives us another year; it is a beautiful gift. It is the gift of life, which we must render back to Him.

This is the moment in which the old touches the new, in which we offer gratitude to God, and also atonement—atonement for our sins and for the sins of the whole world.

This is the moment when we can lift the burden, the heavy burden of guilt and of misery, from the hearts of our brothers and sisters in Christ. So, we spend this time, as much as possible, in prayer, in availability, and in an inward atonement.

Let us ask, this year, that God may grant to the world a year of mercy, a year of love—His love—a year of His peace that no one can take away.

Let us ask for a year of His tenderness, so that we may give tenderness to others; a year of gentleness, so that we may be gentle with others.

And then, let us enter the New Year with hope, knowing that we can do nothing of ourselves. Let us walk in faith, and that faith will grow and grow! And we will begin to understand that *He can do all things in us*.

In total simplicity and childlikeness, in a faith that sings of our desire for Him, in a love that celebrates with an untarnished hope, let us face this New Year without fear!

Why should we be afraid when the Lord is with us? We live in the resurrected Christ. Together, upholding each other in love and joy and faith, we shall restore that which needs restoring in the Church.

Love, as I look at it, is mine to have, and to give; so it is yours for the taking. I give you, in the midst of all the Christmas decorations, my love. And I ask the Lord to give you peace. I pray passionately that you become 'at peace'— first with God, then with yourself, and then with everyone.

May you be gifted this coming year with understanding, tenderness, compassion, forgiveness, reconciliation, faith, hope and love.

I pray that your heart may become more and more like that of the Christ Child. I pray that, through all your years, you will walk close to Our Lady, for the Child came through her, and through her you can go to Him.

January 1
Solemnity of Mary, Mother of God

This holy day falls on the last day of the octave of Christmas, marking the eighth day of celebration of the birth of Christ. Special attention is given to Mary's title of the Mother of God, surely the highest and most significant of her many titles.

This is from one of Catherine's commentaries on a Gospel reading for this day.

What I like about Mary is that (as it says in the text) she "treasured all these things and pondered them in her heart."(Cf. Luke 2:51) The shepherds came to the stable, saw the Child in the manger, and told the Holy Family about the astonishing things they'd heard and seen—angels and all that. Then the shepherds departed from the scene, leaving Mary and Joseph alone to contemplate what had happened.

Right after that, the text says that Mary kept everything in her heart. What a wonderful example of prayer she is for all of us! How many of us have 'taken to heart' the things of God that have been revealed to us? How many of us will treasure in our hearts the things that God is going to reveal to us in the coming year?

Mary, you see, does not exist in isolation. For a Christian, her meaning lies in the fact that, in her, God has realized first and perfectly His design for the whole Church—and for each individual Christian. Whenever we talk about Mary, then, we are ultimately saying something about *ourselves*. And we are proclaiming the Christian idea of what it means to be human, because Mary was the perfect Christian.

The coming of Christ on earth was due to a miraculous intervention by God. Christ came through Mary without the seed of a male, and she remained a virgin. God the Father chose a woman to give us God the Son, through the power of the Holy Spirit. Can any greater honor be given to womanhood? And that woman is Mary! She is Our Lady of the Trinity.

To me, she is like a door that is finely wrought. There is an important symbolism here. I cannot get away from the very simple fact that Christ came to us *through* a woman, *through* Mary. She was the door between heaven and earth.

By her life, by her witnessing, she has become for us the door that leads to the Way, who is Christ. And Christ leads to the Father. And the Holy Spirit walks with us, and helps us not to get off that Way.

Yes, Mary is like a door, or a gate. We sit at her feet, at the gateway, enveloped in her silence. Her silence is filled with the Holy Spirit, and we let that silence penetrate to the marrow of our bones. She is Our Lady of Silence. She is the spouse of the Holy Spirit—the Divine Spouse who leads us to the Son. And the Son leads us to the Father.

Silence must reign where God dwells. And yet the silence of God is somehow thunderous, if we will but listen to it. It comes at first in a whisper. It may come later as rolling thunder. It can come in every which way. However it may speak to us, it behooves us to listen carefully.

Yes, the Woman Wrapped in Silence has a lot to say, if we will sit at her feet and listen.

It is traditional on New Year's day for French-Canadians to make a visit to the patriarch of their family, their father or grandfather, to receive his paternal blessing for the coming year. Members of Madonna House receive this blessing from their priestly spiritual directors.

Feast of the Epiphany

This day is sometimes called Star Christmas or Little Christmas, and is one of the oldest Christian feasts in the Church calendar. It originally was considered as the day of Christ's birth, and it is still celebrated that way in Eastern Churches today. In the Western Church, it has become a movable feast and need not always be on January 6th. In

> *some countries, it is celebrated on the Sunday that falls between January 2nd and 8th.*
>
> *Epiphany is a word that means 'manifestation' or 'showing forth'. It commemorates the manifestations of the divinity of Christ, which are sometimes called Theophany, which means the showing forth of God.*

The event most commonly associated with the Feast of the Epiphany is that of Christ's being 'made visible' to the Magi, the Wise Men who followed a star to Bethlehem. Because of their three gifts for the Christ Child—gold, frankincense, and myrrh—tradition has it that the Wise Men were three in number, and of kingly origin. So they are often called the Three Kings.

But other manifestations of God's Presence are also celebrated on this day. One is the baptism of Christ in the River Jordan by John the Baptist. Another is the miracle of the water being changed into wine by Christ at Cana. Because of this, it is a day on which, in many churches, all the waters of the earth are blessed.

We at Madonna House observe this custom by having a special procession to the Madawaska River. The waters are blessed, and then a crucifix is thrown into the river (through a hole in the ice) so that the Presence of Christ will continue to bless these waters throughout the year.

In the chapel, water is also blest and is used in the coming weeks and months as holy water. It is called Epiphany Water.

After Epiphany Mass and the blessing of the waters, we enjoy a festive breakfast with a special round coffee cake, which has been decorated like a king's crown. There's one cake for each table in our dining room. Hidden inside each of three of these cakes is a bright shiny coin.

A portion of cake is cut and given to each person at the table. As breakfast progresses, more of the cake is eaten. As some point, one table may erupt with cries of delight. A coin has been discovered! And the name of the lucky finder is announced.

Later in the day, the three persons who've found coins will go before the Blessed Sacrament and spend an hour of prayer, asking for God's blessing upon the whole family.

Catherine comments:

Epiphany is such a beautiful feast. It brings everybody together. It is also a very profound feast, for it is the revelation of Christ to the Gentiles. Somewhere, deep in their very hearts, the non-Jews were awaiting Him, expecting Him. It was a strange affair. It always cheered me up to remember this, especially when I was lecturing on interracial justice.

Just think for a moment. Three Wise Men from the East. One was supposed to be a Negro, and the other two were apparently Persians. Three came to worship Him—multicolored, in a manner of speaking.

So did I worship Him. I used to worship Him in a crummy little storefront, with children dancing on the garbage cans amidst all the noise of Harlem.

He revealed Himself to the whole world on Epiphany. Oh, I know there are all kinds of revelations of the Lord. But the *first* one was Epiphany. And I was 'there' with the Magi. I even brought gifts to Him: myrrh of my works, frankincense of my prayers, gold of compassion and understanding that He had put into my heart.

I strewed it all right in front of Him. He was little, but He gathered everything up in His tiny hand, because they were all intangible gifts. It wasn't gold; it wasn't frankincense; it wasn't myrrh. It was *love!* Even when He was little, just barely born, He could put out His little hands and gather it up. It was all so very simple, because He was Love Himself.

The doorways of Madonna House are marked with a house blessing on this day, usually just as we are gathering for our evening meal. This tradition is common in Eastern Europe, from the Baltic Sea down to the Mediterranean. You can adapt this custom for your own home, as follows:

A piece of chalk is first blessed with holy water.

The head of the household takes the chalk and makes an inscription with it on the lintel, just above the main doorway of the house. It should look something like this:

20 † C † B † M † 01

It consists of three initials—which represent the first letters of the names of the Wise Men (traditionally known as Caspar, Balthazar, and Melchior)—enclosed by the numerals of the current year (2001 is shown above), and interspersed with small crosses.

God's blessing is then asked on all who abide in this home, and who pass through its doorways. (If you desire, the prayer can be said alternately by two people.)

Let us pray: O Triune God, may the intercessions of Blessed Caspar, Balthazar and Melchior, and of all the saints, make our prayers acceptable to You. For today, we come before You to dedicate this home to Your service.

All: How good and how pleasant it is, when all live together in unity. (Cf. Psalm 132, 133.)

O Heavenly Father, You wish to come and dwell among Your people on earth, both individually and communally. Build us up into a holy edifice, that we may be one in Your service. Grant that we may become a temple made up of living stones, with the truths of our faith as the foundation, and Your Son, Jesus, as our cornerstone.

All: How good and how pleasant it is, when all live together in unity.

Lord Jesus Christ, you lived in the home of Martha and Mary, and blessed them by Your Presence. Come to our home, too, and make it a dwelling place of Your mercy and peace. Grant that we who abide here may serve You in spirit and in truth, and grow together in an ever-deepening love.

All: How good and how pleasant it is, when all live together in unity.

Holy Spirit, give to those who pass through the doorways of this home a knowledge of Your Presence within their hearts. Bless their coming in, and their going out. Watch over them, wherever they may journey. Guard them, and guide them, in all their words and actions. Give them the yearning hearts of the Wise Kings who came to Bethlehem, so that they may be always on the watch for Your star to guide them.

All: How good and how pleasant it is, when all live together in unity.

May the Divine Presence come down upon this dwelling [sprinkle holy water around the room] to sanctify all that is here. May this saving water cleanse us of our sins and failings, and restore us to wholeness, so that now, and in the days to come, we may celebrate the mercies of the Lord.

All: Amen.

O Holy Trinity, in simplicity of heart we have joyously offered our home and our lives to You. In expectation and delight, we look forward to having You dwell with us, each day of the year.

All: Amen! Amen! Amen!

> *In Russia, one of the ornaments of this season is a star. The Russians made enormous stars and put them over their isbas (log cabins) to represent the star of Bethlehem. Catherine says:*

You know something? If we go out and follow that star, we ourselves will become a star. And others will follow us to that Immense Star that is Christ.

The Star is fire and flame and beauty. It is love and faith and hope. And we can ignite ourselves from Him. The composition of the Star is what we want to become; we want to be like Christ. And, as we follow it, it rubs against us. And here we are, becoming a star ourselves!

But it takes all of our being to follow that star.

On Epiphany evening at Madonna House, just after dessert has been served at the evening meal, three men dressed in kingly robes enter the dining room. They move from table to table with trays of gifts—which are really brightly colored cards, cut into the shape of crowns, stars, camels, or whatever imagination suggests.

On each card is written a word or phrase. The 'kings' let each person pick out a gift, from the many that are available.

But this is done in random fashion, without trying to choose a particular 'word' for oneself.

The word or phrase may be a *virtue* such as faith, hope, charity, fortitude, justice, and so forth. Or else it may be a *quality of soul* such as playfulness, gratitude, perseverance, cheerfulness, simplicity, etc. Throughout the remainder of the year, the recipients are to exercise their particular gifts in the practical work of daily living.

Catherine comments again:

This is the time of bringing gifts to God. God is in our midst, you know: right here, right now! And He can be hurt in each one of us, or He can be consoled in each one of us. Christ said, "Whatever you do to the least of My brothers, you do to Me."

We must learn how to bring the gift of consolation to the Christ in those around us. Whenever we do this, we will be consoling God Himself. To console God, or to hurt Him deeply: what a power we have! What a responsibility!

My good holy mother (God rest her soul) put it in a much more simple way. "Catherine," she said, "You'd better start ransoming Christ. They paid thirty pieces of silver for Him. Now you must make your life such that, at the end of it, you will have ransomed Christ by giving thirty pieces of silver back."

To "ransom" Christ! What a strange expression! And how do I fashion a silver coin out of my daily actions? To this day, I really don't know. But the words of my mother constantly ring in my ears.

I think that ransoming Christ is consoling Christ. I think it means loving my brother or my sister, whoever is around me. Ransoming Christ is loving people—and loving my enemy, too! It is giving my life for another person.

I don't need to be killed for the other. I just give my life in little bits—such tiny little bits. *Listening* is giving my life. *Serving* is giving my life. Such simple things!

And so today, at the beginning of this Year of Grace, when all is uncertain in our strange world, I suggest that, when we pray, we ask God to be able to accept the uncertainties of life without fear. For *'God is with us'* (Emmanuel), and He is our Certainty.

The Feast of the Baptism of the Lord

In the Latin rite, Christ's Baptism is celebrated on the Sunday after Epiphany. With this event, the Christmas cycle comes to a close. Catherine comments:

Now let's see what the Gospel says about Jesus going into the River Jordan, to be baptized by John. (Matt. 3:13–17; Mark 1:6–11; Luke 3:15–22.)

There is a great consolation in these words. John the Baptist, who is one of the last of the prophets (straddling the Old and the New Testaments, in a way) quite naturally says, "It is I who need baptism from You, and yet You come to me." And Jesus replies: "Leave it like this for the time being. It is fitting that we should in this way do all that righteousness demands." Jesus wants to obey the law, so that not a single iota of the law shall be lost.

This should console us, too, in another way. We, who are great sinners, see that the Lord is bending down to wash our feet. And we say to Him, "Lord, it is I who should be washing Your feet." He responds, "No, unless you let Me do it. . . ." and so forth. (Well, that is a consolation, is it not?)

But it is also a challenge to us. If God not only forgives our sins but washes our feet—so that His Law of Love may be fulfilled upon our body, symbolically speaking, as well as in our soul—what are we going to do about it? How are we to conform to this 'new image' of ourselves?

The Baptism of Christ manifests itself before us. Jesus Christ is here before us, washing our feet, just as He allowed Himself to be cleansed in the River Jordan by a sinner named John (who was a saint). You and I have come out of those cleansing waters, along with Christ! We have been made clean; and we have been strengthened by the Holy Spirit.

Though we may have been sinners once upon a time, now we are *saved* sinners! Let us ponder this beautiful mystery of Christ's Baptism, and understand that it means *freedom* for us. Freedom from sin. And especially, freedom from guilt!

Do you remember the freedom song, "We shall overcome"? Sing it to yourself, to remind your heart that you have been made free. "Deep in my heart, I do believe, we shall overcome some day."

But the words themselves are not enough. We have to cooperate with the workings of the Holy Spirit. If we are willing to cooperate with Him, then we will begin to be free. Otherwise, the reign of justice cannot take place within us. And unless it does take place in us, it will not take place in the world either! Unless we cooperate with the Spirit, we *hold back* the reign of justice on earth!

Let us have beautiful eyes, not guilt-dimmed ones, to see what God is trying to make of us: an *icon* of Christ. Let us have beautiful ears, not guilt-stopped ones, to hear His Voice speaking to us.

It has not quite entered into us, as yet, what God is doing. We do not hear the Voice who speaks from Heaven, saying to us always: "This is My Beloved One. My favor rests on Him"—and on *all those who follow Him.*

Book III

Stories

How we love stories! Why are they so powerful in helping us understand and remember deep truths about life? Isn't it because stories are *closer to life* than mere ideas?

Jesus knew this. He, the Master Teacher, told the most beautiful and the most unforgettable stories in the history of the world. They are so deep that they now are woven into the very fiber of our hearts and minds. "In all this teaching to the crowds, Jesus spoke in parables. In fact, he never spoke to them without a parable" (Matt. 13:34).

Stories, then, are simply another way of sharing the understanding of the Gospel with others. That is why Jesus often spoke in story form.

From the very beginning of my apostolic life, I have used stories, and they have been understood and loved by young and old alike. I still continue to speak in stories. They come naturally to me.

I have found, living in this sophisticated, technological generation of today, that the hearts of people still yearn for stories, for explanation of things 'wrapped up' in symbols, which are simple yet somewhat mysterious.

When I was a child, my mother and father taught me by stories. Because I had traveled much during my childhood, these stories were in many languages. And many of them were taken from the folklore of the pilgrims and peasants. Yes, I come from a country and a generation that *listened*, an oral generation in many ways, one that transmitted its lore, history, and traditions through stories and parables.

Most every family has its own tradition of stories that have been told and retold by generations. Some of those stories really happened to the parents or grandparents or distant ancestors. Other stories are beautiful legends or folklore of the nationality to which the family belongs.

These stories flow from the lives and adventures of people on pilgrimage in search of God. The stories are true because their message is true. The rest must be left to the heart of each reader.

Whether factual or legendary, these stories should truly be cherished because they are the very soul of a family's tradition and continuity. They help to create and perpetuate a close 'family feeling' between young members and older ones, and between all living family members and those who have gone before them to their eternal rest. Through traditional family stories, these ancestors live, once again, in the bosom of the family.

Perhaps your family has a story or two that you can tell to one another. It may be a humorous story, or one with religious significance. Children love stories; and even adults rarely tire of hearing a good tale well told. In today's world, it costs little to tell a story—simply some 'family time' together.

The Christmas Gift

The following story took place when Catherine was living and working in the slums of Toronto in the 1930's, at the first Friendship House. She was assisted by Franciscan tertiaries, who were lay people following in the footsteps of St. Francis of Assisi. Today such people are called Third Order Franciscans or members of the Secular Franciscan Order.

Catherine, herself, was such a tertiary, and she and her workers at Friendship House helped transient people, whom Catherine always called the 'Brothers Christopher'. Settle back now and listen, as Catherine tells us the tale of a long-ago Christmas.

Outside, the late October evening was dark and stormy. Snow and sleet fell on almost deserted streets. The north wind seemed to take delight in squeezing itself into all the crevices and holes the houses possessed.

The big front room of Friendship House was warm and cozy. The Quebec heater roared contentedly, its big belly filled to the top with glowing warm coals. The large kettle on its top sang its happy song invitingly, and reminded everyone that here was nice tea to be had at any time.

Around the large table full of Catholic magazines and newspapers were sitting several workers who had dropped in to get the latest news. Others were wandering around the bookshelves that covered the four walls, inspecting, looking for some good book to take home with them. At a large desk one of the tertiaries was deeply engrossed in writing an article, and the uneven noise of the typewriter blended with the wind and storm and the roaring heater made the place more alive.

From the next room, a kitchen, came the clatter of tea cups and the subdued laughter of other tertiaries who were preparing a little lunch for the study group, which could be heard occasionally discussing sociology and liturgy. The whole picture was quiet and peaceful.

Suddenly the front door opened with a wrench, letting in a blast of cold air, snow and rain, and the dark figure of a man stood for a moment framed against the outside darkness, almost a part of it. Then, slamming the door with a bang, he riveted his eyes on a large crucifix before which burned dimly a little red votive lamp.

"Another hell-hole of a Christian place!" the man shouted. "Just my luck. I have been thrown out of three tonight, and I am sick, tired, cold and hungry! I was told that there was a communist hall this way, and I had to land here instead."

Quietly, the tertiary who had been typing stood up, a tall figure in a simple brown dress with a silver crucifix gleaming dully in the light. Smilingly, she advanced toward the man and, stretching out her hand, said, "It might be a hell-hole, for we are very poor and have little to offer. It is a Christian place also; but we will not tell you to leave. On the contrary, we welcome you to stay with us as long as you need.

"Forgive our poverty, and share what God in His mercy has seen fit to send us. I am sure He guided you to us; the communist hall is only a few steps down." With these words she approached the man.

He looked a little bewildered, then he took a deep breath and collapsed at her feet. Everyone helped to raise him, and he was quickly taken upstairs where a tertiary brother helped him to a warm bath and gave him some dry clothes, for all he had was a jersey, a pair of trousers and some old tennis shoes, and these were soaked.

Clean and warm, he came down to a nice warm lunch prepared quickly for him. But he remained sullen and silent. From the few disjointed sentences he muttered, the tertiaries understood that he was a transient, that he had overstayed his 24-hour city ticket and therefore was not entitled anymore to either food or shelter at the city hostels and had to move on.

Yet, in his flimsy garment, and with the coming storm, he had tried the private agencies. But they were either full, or had so much red tape attached to their admission that he gave up. And in the last one, he expressed himself rather forcefully and had simply been thrown out.

So he had continued wandering. He was looking for a communist shelter—first, because he called himself a communist, and secondly because he knew that "they wouldn't throw even a dog out in such weather."

Without commenting, the tertiaries listened to this short, disjointed yet pitiful tale. They had learned from long and bitter experience that in such cases little would be achieved by words, and more by silence and prayer. Seeing his utter exhaustion, they advised him to go to sleep and discuss things more fully on the morrow.

Tomorrow came. But the man sat sullen and silent in his corner. Only his dark eyes were alive, observing all that was going on. In the light of day, he appeared slight, with an intellectual face, young, not over 30. The tertiaries left him alone all day, and only smiled encouragingly as they passed by.

Toward the evening he stepped up to one of them and wanted to know what was he supposed to do in exchange for his shelter and food. "Nothing," answered the woman. "Nothing, my friend. You are a guest of St. Francis here; we are only his humble servants. There is nothing you *have* to do. Just rest and get strong, look for work, or let us look for you.

"Everything in this place belongs to you and your brothers, the 'Christophers' (Christ-bearers) of our great roads. We are only stewards of this place, and our greatest privilege is to help and serve people like you. If, at any time, you want a part in our lives, and want to help us to help others like you, let us know and we will find some work for you to do. But there is no obligation of any kind."

The man did not answer, but once again an expression of astonishment and childish bewilderment passed across his face.

Days merged into weeks and still John (he had given no other name and none was asked of him) sat quietly in his corner, a silent listener to all the discussions and con-versations that were continually taking place at Friendship House. Intensely he observed how the tertiaries dealt with the many clients of St. Francis, who came in an endless stream, begging for food, clothing, moral and material help.

Occasionally he smiled a funny, angry, crooked smile when someone would suggest *praying* for the coffee that was getting low, or *asking St. Francis* to send coal, which was badly needed. Yet, little by little, as the coffee came and the coal arrived, the smile vanished from his face to be replaced by a puzzled look of concentration, as if he were trying to understand something that eluded his mind.

At the beginning of the third week, he sat before the tertiary's desk and resolutely told her that, since he was a communist, he desired to attend their meetings—and would she object to it?

Sorrowfully, she lifted her face and answered: "No, you can do what you want, John. I will only ask you never to discuss what you hear there with anyone here during my absence. It wouldn't be fair to the others, would it?" He agreed that it would not and that he would not do so.

From that time on, he was often absent half of the day. But he was always home for supper, after which the tertiaries would ask him what he had heard that day at his communist meetings. He would answer and there would start a long discussion, point by point, of the Catholic views as opposed to those of communism. Catholic papers would come out, and books would be piled high on the table, in substantiation of this point or that.

John ceased to be silent. He became the center of all conversations, stimulating others and arguing with them, drawing all present into the fray.

One day, he carried away a bunch of Catholic papers that dealt with a social question being discussed, and informed everybody at large that he was "taking a few papers to my friends the communists" because "they need broadening out."

"There's a lot of sense to the encyclicals, and they'd better hear some of it." On this remark, he slammed the door and left, leaving everyone a little dizzy at the prospect of a communist teaching the encyclicals of the popes to another group of communists. But the ways of God are incomprehensible to man.

A few days later, on a Sunday, while the tertiaries were bemoaning the absence of one of their group, which made them short-handed for the sale of the Catholic paper at the church door, John cheerfully offered to replace him. A few moments later, John was lustily calling out: "Buy a Catholic paper! Help us to do Catholic Action to offset communist and atheist action!" He whistled a joyful tune on the way home and saw nothing out of the way in his method of action, dismissing all thanks with a "one good turn deserves another."

During that time, John—of his own volition—took in hand the distribution of work to those of the 'Brothers Christopher' who evinced a desire to help. Soon, the house shone like a jewel: windows were polished, floors scrubbed, and the cook wore a happy smile because of some new cheap recipe John had dug up. The dishwashers were through in half the time, thanks to a new soap solution he invented.

Everyone agreed he was efficient, and he smilingly called it his "communist technique." The tertiaries just as smilingly answered that he had "become Catholic after a while."

Once, when the place was empty of visitors and friends, he asked a tertiary why they devoted their lives to the poor when they all could have good jobs. Why were they living in the slums when their families had lovely homes? Why this simple hospitality—which asked no questions, nor any return? Why this eternal begging for others—so hard and so difficult?

Gently, the tertiary looked into his eyes and slowly answered: "Today's are tragic days when people have forgotten God. And because of that, some who still remember Him have left their homes and friends to live among the needy and poor. They come to help them, to share with them their life of hardship, to atone for the rich who have forgotten their 'brothers and sisters', the poor, who must carry the heavy load which the greed and injustice of their fellow men have thrust upon them.

"Not all are called to a life like this. But those who have this vocation are privileged and rich beyond the dreams of men, for they do it out of love of Christ, whom they see in the poor and down-trodden. It's all really very simple, and so very wonderful."

For a moment both remained silent. Then John told her that he was born a Catholic, and that he had a brother who was a priest. At an early age he had left home and wandered to many places, but he'd always kept his faith—until he began to work for a selfish Catholic employer, whose greed made hundreds of his workers miserable and unhappy. Watching all this, John had lost his faith and had joined the communist party.

As John finished speaking, he suddenly jumped up, grabbed his hat and was gone. That evening, many prayers were said for him, and for the many tired 'lost souls' like him.

Christmas was coming. And in the hustle and bustle of preparing a little feast for 600 children, and a Christmas dinner for the many Brothers Christopher, the tertiaries forgot about John a little. Besides, they knew he'd found a job and another place to live, and now visited Friendship House rarely.

Christmas Eve came. As everyone was making ready to go to Midnight Mass, John walked in and announced that he had brought a Christmas present to them, but he would give it later. Everyone thanked him, but suggested that he had not worked long enough to allow himself the luxury of buying Christmas presents. John only smiled.

In the rush to get to Mass on time, John was lost sight of. Suddenly, in the church, one of the tertiaries excitedly pointed out to the others a man getting out of the confessional—it was John. Astonished, and glad beyond words, the tertiaries rendered thanks to God; it was with tears of happiness that they saw John approach the communion rail.

Later, on their way home under the starry winter sky, he said: "This is my Christmas present to you. I had ceased to believe in God, but I saw Him living and walking again in the Toronto slums. *You* showed Him to me." All remained silent, for they knew what a great miracle had taken place, and that indeed the Christ Child had sent them a most wonderful gift—but they had done so little to deserve it.

Once more, they realized that the ways of God are incomprehensible, and they rendered thanks. Today, John works in a distant northern mining camp. He is a real apostle of Christ and the spirit of St. Francis lives in him. Many are the souls he has brought back to God.

Let us never forget that around us there are thousands of men like John, and that a kind word or a kind gesture might make the difference between a saved soul or a lost one. Let us therefore remember to love our fellow men as St. Francis used to love them, and leave the rest to God's grace.

Christmas Without Christ

> *What was your most memorable Christmas? Was it when you were very little? Was it when you did not have what you wished for at Christmas-time? Was it when you were together or apart from your loved ones? Did you have an unexpected guest or event one Christmas? Catherine was once asked about her most memorable Christmas. Her answer is told in the following story:*

People talk and write of revolutions, and those who read about them sometimes foolishly wish that they lived in a country and at a time when such exciting events took place, for it all seems packed with great excitement and adventure. But take it from me, who went through one of the most tragic revolutions of history—the communist one in Russia—that there is little excitement in them, and less adventure.

Revolutions are composed of tiny little things, which gather together like many little dark clouds to form a huge black one that blots out the sun and the moon and the stars. This leaves you utterly alone in a darkness so dark that you feel you would give your whole life for just *one ray of sunshine.*

Take streets for instance. Old familiar and beloved streets, that you walked all your life. Why yes, at this corner stood your mother, holding your hand to cross the intersection when you were starting kindergarten. And here is the corner store where you bought candies with the hot dirty little pennies that you had clutched so carefully all the way from grade school.

And there is the familiar alley that you always took from high school, because it was a short cut, and because there was a big lilac bush that smelled so nice and made you think of spring and vacations. And a little further was that puppy that you played with, and which now is a nice big woolly dog that still knows you and comes out sedately and slowly to greet you.

Would you believe that all these familiar streets, which you love and remember from almost babyhood, can change overnight into sinister frightening places where death stalks and life is cheap? Yes, that is just what happened after the communist revolution came to 'my streets' in Petrograd.

I was barely 21 when I found out the change. Mother had sent me to see if I could buy some food somewhere. It was early evening. I walked the familiar streets without fear. I loved them, even then when they were dark (the electrical power was off in the city, due to the revolution). Then I stumbled over something. And when I bent down to see what it was, it was a dead woman with a knife in her back, and blood all over the pavement. That was the beginning of the change on my streets.

Then the edict went out that anyone found worshiping God in any church could be shot on sight or arrested. And my streets became jungles to be crossed carefully, slowly, hiddenly, hugging the walls of buildings so as to melt with their shadows in the early morning when going to Mass.

As soon as that edict went out, church services became the center of all life. How long would it be before there would be no Mass? People asked themselves that question, and the thought froze all Christian hearts. For what is life without Mass, without the sacraments?! Men, women and youth arose and went to Mass daily. So did I.

We all went. But we first blessed ourselves *in the name of the Father and the Son and the Holy Spirit*, because we all knew that maybe this was the last time we might walk the familiar yet now unfamiliar streets. We walked as Indians must have when stalking their prey—soft-footed, alert, listening for any loud footsteps. Only communists walked loudly through the fearsome streets.

We walked in human fear, in trembling, but we *had* to go where we were going. To Mass! To Church! Because, *without* it, we would not be able to face another day of wondering, fearing that it would be our last day.

This is another fact about revolutions: they bring 'eternity' into every hour of every day. You peel potatoes in your kitchen and—hark! There are heavy footsteps on the stairs. Are they for you? Are the communist secret police coming to arrest you? Or those you love?

No—they passed your door.

With a trembling hand, you go on peeling potatoes, listening, listening, and wondering about life and death. God is very near then. In fact, *God alone matters*, and so does the Mass.

So we went at dawn, like the Christians of old, softly, hugging walls, watching, now melting with the shadows, now moving, inch by inch, into a dark church.

One day it happened! It happened in church. It was an old church with a cold stone floor—without lights, except for the tabernacle light and two slender candles. It happened right after the consecration, while the priest's hands were still raised high to allow us all, who were living under a 'sentence of death' as it were, to behold Him who died for love of us, and to give us courage if the need arose, to try to die as gallantly for the love of Him.

White were the hands of the priest. White was the Host, shining white were the candles—dark and dim the church—when suddenly the side door opened with a bang and rough voices shouted "Stand still!"

The priest froze with the Host still lifted high. We became statues of immobility lost in the dimness of the church.—Soldiers! for that is who they were. Red Army soldiers.

One of them slowly lifted his rifle and slowly took aim. One shot rang out. Only one. The priest quivered, swayed and fell sideways. The consecrated Host rolled down, down the steps, onto the floor, coming to rest, still and white, on the dark floor by the altar railing—in two pieces.

Silence took over, only to be broken and shattered by the rhythmic steps of the hobnailed boots of the soldiers walking toward the tabernacle, then vaulting over the railing. Triumphantly their voices suddenly rang out while one of them crushed the consecrated Host under his heel: "There is no God! We have crushed Him."

Silence wrapped up his voice and killed it. Silence. The silence of Golgotha entered the church. It hung—even like Christ on the cross—only to be broken again by the thin, reedy voice of an old, old man who spoke from the intense shadows of the church. "Father, forgive them, even if they know what they do."

The silence came back once more—a new silence of mercy and pardon. The Red Army soldiers shivered a little and slowly slunk away through the sacristy. Their hobnailed boots made dragging sounds that were like a dirge. A door slammed in the back. A moan went through the church—our moan of pain and horror.

Slowly, the old man arose. He was a patriarchal figure, with a long white beard and flowing hair. Reverently he gathered the crushed pieces of the consecrated Host. Slowly he bade us to come forward and to receive them in our last communion. Maybe our viaticum. We did.

Then we got holy water and scrubbed the floor. And we stayed on, to pray in reparation. We buried the priest secretly. He was the last priest in town; there would be no Mass, no sacraments.

The familiar streets were still filled with danger and death for us. We didn't mind them anymore, because we ourselves were filled with such desolation, a desolation that no one knows, in countries where there are so many churches and so many priests.

All this happened just before Christmas. And so it was a Christmas without Christ in the tabernacle—without Mass—without confession—without communion.

Just the same, it was my most memorable Christmas. Since they had closed all the doors against His coming, He chose the humble stables of our pain-filled hearts in which to be born anew that strange, lonely, cold Christmas of the first year of the communist Russian Revolution in 1917.

Sometimes it seems to me to have been the most blessed Christmas of all because, from that day on, I knew that, when all the rest had been taken away from me, nothing mattered but His inner presence in my heart.

I wish—oh, how I wish!—that I really could tell all this to all the youth in North America. To so many of them, going to Mass on Sundays seems, at times, too dull and hard. Mass on Sunday? Oh, my friends, go to Mass *every day*—while you can!

Yes, we would have *crawled on our knees* that Christmas—through the strange and fearsome streets, filled with dangers and death—if only we could have participated in just one more Mass.

Thank God each day that, as yet, your most memorable Christmas is not without Christ in all the tabernacles of your many churches.

How Pride Became Humble

The story below is a parable, one of many that Catherine made up 'on the spot' as she was nursing a guest who stayed for a while at Madonna House. The guest was a young contemplative monk whose doctor had advised a change of environment for several months.

After a spell of sickness, when the guest was resting, he would say, "Tell me a story." This is one of the stories Catherine told him, just before he fell asleep.

Lady Pride was born proud. She never remembered a time when she had not been filled with an overwhelming admiration for herself. She passed through the ages, brimful with arrogance, like people who are *sure* that they are better, more clever, and in every way superior to others. She always held her beautiful head very high, and she walked slowly, majestically, across the centuries.

She did not bother to deal with each person to the same degree. While she influenced all, she chose her 'select company' very carefully. If she liked someone, she'd come and stay with that person for a long, long time, and everyone would soon see her influence. People imitated her quite well. They, like her, became cold, aloof and unapproachable, behaving as if they were set apart somehow, and were above the common lot of humans.

Despite her disposition, she was quite beautiful. Her beauty could not be denied. She was tall and stately, and with features that could be called 'classical' by those who know about such things. Yet people, by and large, were afraid of her and of her beauty. There was something about it that was evil, dark, sinister. It reminded them of deep, still, stagnant waters, greenish in color, that could not sustain life but only killed it. All living things died in such waters.

Anyone who has traveled can observe the desolate landscapes created by such waters. Gray, lifeless trees lift their leafless arms to heaven as if crying out from strange depths. The shores are bereft of flowers or grass; they are covered only with sand and rocks. Water plants refuse to take root. Such waters are dead—dead and frightening.

It was of such scenes that people thought whenever they saw Lady Pride pass by. They shivered and turned away. And yet they knew that she often showered her gifts upon her friends. Gold and silver seemed to be hers to give. Power followed in her wake. But it was a darksome power, and it only served her and her friends, those who were slaves to her whims.

Lady Pride often recalled her many conquests; in one event, she took special pride. It had happened a long time ago, perhaps on, or near, the day she was born. It had been an extraordinary day, for she never remembered ever having been young, on that day or any other. She had been born mature.

It was the day on which God—He Who Is—had revealed his secret to the angels. After he had revealed it to them, they were all enthralled, and they remained very, very still.

Lady Pride had not heard the secret herself, but she saw one beautiful spirit (who seemed all-light) begin to frown. He was so beautiful that she desired to be with him forever. She walked softly over to him and whispered to him that, whatever the secret was, it was not for him (for she saw that he did not like what he had heard).

Why should he accept? He was, she convinced him, as great as God himself! The angel of light turned, saw her, and believed what she said.

Then, rising to an immense height, he shouted for all to hear the Motto of Pride: *Non serviam!*—"I will not serve!" Many of the lesser angels joined him after they, too, had looked at Lady Pride.

There ensued a battle that rocked the heavens. For once, Lady Pride put aside her dignity, and joined in the battle—on the side of Lucifer, the Angel of Light.

Suddenly, in the midst of the battle, she stood still. She beheld an awesome and frightening thing. Light was leaving the angel of light and darkness was entering into him. His beauty remained, but now it was a dark beauty—the beauty of deadliness—a travesty of all beauty. One contact with it spelled death forever.

Immediately, Lucifer and his armies fell down, down, down—into depths that Lady Pride had never known to exist! She followed them; but she could not remain in hell. She was earthly as well as hellish.

As the centuries rolled on, she would go back to hell now and then for a visit. Satan still fascinated her. But she like to remain on the earth, where she allowed herself to be used by Satan, whenever he wished.

Perhaps that is another reason why people are always afraid of her. Who can tell? Maybe too, they remembered her part in the fall of their first parents.

Naturally, Lady Pride was there too, in the garden with the snake. It seemed as if her sole purpose of existence was to extend the awful domain of the Angel of Light, the one who had become now the Prince of Darkness!

One starry night Lady Pride was walking, in her slow, majestic fashion. She paused now and then to admire her own reflection in the various lakes, rivers, and pools that dotted her way. She found herself on the outskirts of a small village, the entrance to which was a narrow path. On both sides of the path were caves, dug into the sandy rock which covered the countryside.

One cave especially attracted her attention. It seemed to cast a blinding light onto the path. A great star hovered over it, almost touching the roof. Lady Pride drew closer, pausing now and then, as if afraid to get too close.

The wooden door of the cave was full of chinks and holes. It was just an old stable door. The cave was used, it seemed, only to house animals. Lady Pride was, for once, unsure of herself, and strangely troubled.

Then, slowly, she opened the door, not really expecting to see anyone. On the contrary, she saw a woman holding a Child in her arms! And there was a man kneeling in seeming adoration. The man got up and made a step or two toward the door, as if to bar the way. But the woman shook her head gently, so the man stopped.

Lady Pride entered and gently closed the door behind her. The woman, a mere child herself, seemed to grow taller and more mature as she held up the Child and sang this song of praise:

"My soul praises the Lord; my soul is glad because of God my Savior. For He has remembered me, His lowly servant! And from now on all people will call me blessed."

Lady Pride fell on her knees. Suddenly she knew that *this was the sight that God had shown the angels* on the day she was born. She had not seen it then. She had only seen the frown of Lucifer, the Prince of Pride. It was this Child she had counseled him not to serve.

With her head in the straw which littered the floor, Lady Pride wept. She wept bitter, scalding tears of sorrow and compunction. She wished she were dead. She wished she had never been born. She wished she had never seen Lucifer or spoken to him. The enormity of her offense stood out so clearly that she was blinded by the sight.

But the Lady with the Child was smiling again. And, though Lady Pride did not hear any words spoken, she knew that she had been forgiven and that, henceforth, she would never be the same.

She had beheld with her own eyes the fullness of *Truth Incarnate*, God made flesh—God and his Mother! And that is how Lady Pride became humble.

Today, she takes pride only in the works of God, especially those wonders of grace He accomplishes in the hearts of men.

Lucifer wept too—but with anger. He picked up Haughtiness, which Lady Pride had left on the straw of the cave, and he made it his own. Thus it is today that, when people see a cold and haughty beauty walking the earth, one who 'puts on' a great arrogance and an insufferable pride, they see a ghostly reflection of the heart of Lucifer, the Angel of Light who became the Prince of Darkness.

The Bruised Reed

The following story is a Christmas fable, written by Jude Fischer, a staff worker of Madonna House. It is one of a collection of stories excerpted from her book, Be Always Little.

Once there was a reed, tall and proud, growing near a stream. He was a fine reed indeed. And how he loved life! He lived every moment to the full! From his height, he had a splendid view of the whole area.

He watched the small animals scampering to and fro, the birds darting here and there, the multi-hued insects, the fish gliding in the stream. Best of all, he liked the flowers. They came in a never-ending parade of exquisite form and color. Old friends would go; but new ones promptly followed and delighted him so, that he never stopped to wonder what happened to the old. And all the while he stood tall and green. Yes, life was good indeed.

One morning he awoke, and as he looked into the stream he discovered that his tip was turning brown. His dismay grew as, day after day, the malady spread until his fine green coat was completely gone. Not only that, he began to feel dry, then drier and drier.

The rains came and beat at him; the wind battered him; and finally a mighty gust snapped him loose from the earth. He lay desolate on the ground—broken, bruised, and heavy-hearted.

Some days later, a young man came by and picked him up. He put him in his bag. It was black inside, so black that the poor reed could see nothing at all. He longed for the end, for *anything* but this unending darkness.

Finally the day came when the young man took him out of the bag. How good it was to see light again! And he saw fields and rolling hills and sheep grazing peacefully around. The young man took a sharp knife and cut part of Reed away, hurting him so acutely he couldn't help but cry out. Then the man ruthlessly pierced him through, from end to end, clearing out his hollow. Every inch of his being quivered with pain. Then he was thrust back into the darkness again.

Sometime later he was taken out. He welcomed the light, yet dreaded the pain he anticipated would come along with it. And sure enough, there was the knife. This time the young man mercilessly cut several holes in him. He wept silently. Then he was plunged once more into blackness.

The day came when Reed, from his dark home in the bag, sensed something different, some excitement in the air. The young man joined some other shepherds and they hurried toward the edge of town. There they went into a cave, and the young man pulled Reed out of the bag. Reed braced himself for the inevitable knife.

Instead, to his surprise, he felt only the gentle caress of the young man's hands as he lifted him tenderly to his lips. Then the young man poured his life's breath into him; and there came forth from Reed a beautiful song, simple and pure.

And as Reed sang, he looked out and saw a young mother and her little Baby. And they smiled at him.

"The people walking in darkness have seen a great light" (Isa. 9:1).

A Woman, a Child, and Christmas

Many stories that Catherine told were true. They were actual incidents taken from her years of living and working with the poor, first in Toronto, then in New York's Harlem section, in Chicago and other cities.

She called these her 'Blue Door Stories' since the doors of Friendship House and later, Madonna House, were always painted blue, in honor of Our Lady. This lovely custom comes from an old Russian saying that "Every front door painted blue in honor of Our Lady brings blessings on all who pass through it."

The story below was a true happening of God's mercy— what Raïssa Maritain, a good friend of Catherine's, would call an 'adventure in grace'!

His shoulders were thin and hunched over, like those of a man who never in his life had a warm coat to shield him against the biting winds. It was as if he had always tried to make himself narrow so there would be less for the wind to whip around.

His face was long, thin and sort of transparent. His eyes were blank and terrible to behold. He was like a blind man who was seeing. Emptiness, with endless frightened depths, could be found in those eyes, if you looked long enough. But few bothered.

He made his way to the Quebec heater in the middle of our big room. Taking off his hat, he twisted it absent-mindedly in his hands, which were extended toward the pleasant heat of the strong fire. The men looked up from their game of cards, or from their newspapers and magazines. All sort of nodded or smiled. He did not seem to notice. He just stood there, twisting his hat as before, hunching his thin shoulders, and warming himself.

I got up and made my way to the man. I asked if he was hungry. He nodded yes, as if he was too tired to speak. I led him to the back room, our kitchen, and placed some food before him. He sat down. He ate wolfishly, as one who needed food desperately.

Then suddenly he wept, with deep, racking sobs that foretold the rushing waters of a dam about to break. I sat still. The pain of Christ encompassed me as it had for years. Thousands like him who had come through the Blue Door had brought His pain to me, to us, that we might take it away from them, and take it into ourselves. That is what loving the neighbor really means—becoming the bearer of their cross of pain, sorrow and need.

Then, just as suddenly as he had begun to cry, he began to speak. The story he told was a simple one, sordid and old, yet somehow poignant, new, full of pain. For when a story is connected with a human being, with *real* life, it is never old, or sordid, or simple.

He had married much too young. She became pregnant. He, in turn, became frightened of the poverty all around them. He abandoned her. That was six months ago.

After that, he found that he could not live with himself. He went back because she was alone, young and defenseless. All around about was the Great Depression. No jobs. But he had returned too late. She had vanished and left no trace, at least none that he could follow.

After that, he did not care. He became a sort of bum, riding the rails—but always in search of her—his abandoned wife—and the child. The baby should by now be several weeks old.

Where was she? Where were they, on this Christmas Eve, the feast of babies and of mothers? He lay slumped, his head in pieces of bread and peanut butter, the upset bowl of soup trickling its contents onto his thin overcoat and onto his tightly clenched hands.

A naked heart is difficult to look at. I left him for a while. Later I saw him warming himself by the stove. His eyes were dry again.

Slowly the place emptied out. It was Christmas Eve. One by one the tired and weary, the young and old, the poor and destitute—and those who had become poor for love of them—all were going to Midnight Mass in a nearby church. The young man with the empty eyes did not move. So I decided to stay and share his loneliness and his emptiness. There was always the morning Mass to go to.

A strange, hushed silence settled upon us. I put out most of the lights and put on the lights of the big Christmas tree that stood by our large window. The place looked a little bit like a chapel, with its votive lamp and Christmas lights. Then I lit the lonely candle in the other window as a welcome to wayfarers, another custom of my faraway country.

Still the young man did not move. Slowly I began my rosary. What else could I do before the silent drama of a man's soul on this holy night but pray? The snow was falling fast and heavy. Hurrying passersby were but shadows outside the warm circle of our room.

Without warning, the door opened. A woman with a baby wrapped in a shawl stood there, framed like a picture, the snowflakes on her melting quickly in the heat. I stood up to greet her, but the young man was quicker. He had turned and had seen her.

He almost *jumped* the space that separated them. She was quickly in his arms. He was repeating the woman's name over and over again. The baby began to cry. Then everything was silent.

The statue of the Blessed Virgin, with the votive lamp flickering on her face, seemed to come alive. The silence was profound. Then the bells of the church nearby rang out their glad news of the birth of the Child.

The thin man with the hunched shoulders had found her whom his heart was seeking. I gently closed the Blue Door the woman had left open in her excitement, and I went into the kitchen to finish my rosary.

First Christmas in Combermere

Catherine and Eddie came to Combermere in the spring of 1947. Their first winter there was a difficult one, with much snow and cold weather, long before others came to join them—save for Grace Flewwelling, or 'Flewy' as she was called.

That first Christmas at Madonna House was a memorable one for them, despite the hardships. For anyone without the means to buy expensive gifts or food for their loved ones, this story is an inspiration.

Catherine tells what it was like in her account below:

The first Christmas of Madonna House was in 1947, and Lady Poverty dwelt with us in her all-shining reality. Madonna House then was just a little six-room house with no out-buildings, except for an outdoor toilet! It stood rather lonely, in what then was a huge, five-acre expanse of white, sparkling snow.

Nature provided us with many splendid evergreens to decorate the house (which we did!) with fragrant greens and a freshly cut Christmas tree.

But absent were the usual shining baubles, the kind that bring delight to the hearts of children (both the real ones and the ones whose heads might be gray with age).

There were just Eddie, myself, and Flewy (our first staff worker here). Flewy's hands worked wonders with the little humble things that we had for decorating our tree, which stood in the corner of the little room with the fireplace, over-looking the river.

A few walnuts had been donated to us, about a pound or so. And Flewy, who was an artist, painted them with some old gold and silver paint, which she'd brought with her from Harlem. We put hair pins into them and hung them on the tree with black threads.

Flewy then cut a roll of donated tinfoil into artistic shapes, mostly liturgical symbols such as the Infant and His mother, St. Joseph, oxen, donkeys and stars. Those we hung on the tree too. A few other little donated odds and ends we fashioned into ornaments, and topped it off with candles, since we had no electric lights.

I was reminded of our trees in Russia, which were always lit with candles. There is nothing to replace the soft, wonder-ful glow of candles, as long as one is careful and watchful of them!

Flewy's ingenuity—and the lovely, fresh greens, little bits of ribbon and whipped up 'snow' made from soap—complet-ed our decor. I think we did very well, although decorating in the usual fancy, delightful Christmas style we were accus-tomed to was impossible.

Flewy took the china crucifix and made a lovely display, putting in a little statue of the Madonna with a Baby in her arms, which we had around the house. Then she lit a votive light before it. In its soft glow, the tender little bit of tinsel we'd found in a carton just glowed, and its bluish-silver color came out, giving the whole room a real Christmas feeling.

Since I am reminiscing, I'll tell you the story of that Italian china crucifix, the one that still stands today over the fireplace. I used to work at a large department store in Toronto, in its gift shop, which was a place of bedlam at

Christmas time, a place where sales clerks got tired to the point of exhaustion.

I was unwrapping things in the stock room when I came to that crucifix. It slipped from my tired fingers and broke in a couple of pieces. You can still see the breakage. Christmas spirit or no Christmas spirit, the head of the department charged me the full price—*twenty-five dollars!* It was taken out of my $12.50 salary—on which lived a sick husband and a little baby, not counting myself—at one dollar per week for twenty-five weeks.

We all felt the tremendous sting of that missing dollar! But since I was paying for it in full, the crucifix was given to me—forever a memorial of God's grace in allowing me to participate in His poverty on the cross, and His pain.

Flewy and I made wreaths. They were very simple, and we decorated them with pine cones, painted laboriously with some donated red, green, and white paint.

Those were the only decorations for that first Christmas. But words cannot express how great was the love that went into it. How tremendous that first Christmas was, when, after our humble but loving preparations, we went off to Midnight Mass, walking across the road to the church, on a starry night that was rather cold.

The crunching snow was a song in our ears; sweetly it sang its carols to us. The ice on the river reflected the stars and the snow reflected thousands of sparkling stars. As we approached the church, which was softly lighted with kerosene lamps and candles, it glowed like a jewel in the night, and the sound of the choir singing carols greeted us.

It was a Mass I'll never forget, because it was a Mass of joy and great thanksgiving for the gift of the vocation, for the coming of poverty, for the sharing in the life of those we had come to serve, and for the beauty round about us and the charity of God and His tenderness.

It was wonderful to return home and to have our little collation—the Christmas foods that had been laid out on a table in the little library. As we ate, the logs in the fireplace were crackling and singing their carols too.

We had no turkey. We had no goose. We had no ducks. Not even a roast with Yorkshire pudding. We had hamburgers and French fried potatoes, warmed in the oven, and a little plum pudding that I had made—just enough for three.

There was no wine, so we drank tea. But I think all three of us were drunk with joy and gratitude and love!

The gifts we exchanged were nothing in themselves—silly, little, funny things—but lovingly wrapped in beautiful parcels, as beautiful as our love for one another could make it.

We didn't have many items of clothing, so we took from the second-hand pile a sweater not too much worn, a pair of socks for Eddie without too many holes, a warm shirt for him and some warm underwear for us. All had been washed, cleaned and wrapped up very well. The wrapping was our little carol of love to one another, since the rest was given by Our Lady through the charity of others.

We had great joy and much laughter opening our gifts. Flewy received a brooch, not very new, in the shape of a teapot, because she was always going around saying: "That last meal we had was not very filling. How about filling our tummies with a nice, hot, strong cup of tea?" She sure was a great tea drinker.

And the little brooch she gave me was in the shape of a kitchen spoon. I laughed until tears rolled down my cheeks, because I was forever stirring up some 'gook' or other, a creative mixture of unknown leftovers. And we gave Eddie a little one-inch hatchet because, in those days, he was dealing with the splitting and carrying of wood.

I think, amidst our laughter, we were very mature that moment, for we were very childlike and simple. And the spirit of Madonna House with its love for little things was palpable and could have been touched at that moment on that first Christmas—like a living thing—like a living flame among us.

This is how traditions and family customs are established—out of something intangible, out of laughter, out of a joyous minute or hour, out of the wonderment of a human soul at the tremendous gift of childlikeness.

That state of soul, that state of mind, that state of emotion is a gift of God. This is His way of making thin the veil of faith. This is His tender manner of bringing us to Bethlehem, to the manger, to the stupendous, awesome mystery of Jesus Christ—God-made-man!

Your family may not have much this Christmas. But the ingenuity of love, the joy of giving yourselves, each to the other, will far outshine any silly baubles bought with money alone. For the love of Christ is what Christmas is all about, and loving one another will please the Infant inestimably more than any other gift you could possibly dream of.

We didn't have much for ourselves, that Christmas in Combermere. But we had been able to beg a few gifts for our neighbors, though we didn't know many of them the first year here. The closest families to us received our humble, begged gifts of love.

Yes, it was a good Christmas, that first Christmas at Madonna House.

The Little Christmas Angel O'Ryan

The tale below was written by master storyteller Eddie Doherty. This warm, Irish yarn is read to the Madonna House family a few days before Christmas, when there are always guests present.

'Tis a story the Irish, and them of Irish blood, tell their children on Advent nights, when the stars shine brightest and little eyes grow biggest with the wonder of the Christ Child's borning.

'Tis the story of the Angel O'Ryan, a wee cherub not long from his mother's milk, and as holy and zealous and curious a spirit as any newly-ordained priest. Aye, and just as ignorant of the world.

Some hold that he was called after the star *Orion*, the great constellation venerated by race after race of ancient savages. But there are others—and their name is legion—who insist that his mother (God rest her soul!), who was guardian angel to the O'Ryan's in Donegal, had named him after one of the clan.

Be that as it may, the story has it that O'Ryan, within a year of his weaning, was given permission to visit the earth by himself, and to have a look around as part of his angelic education. Sure, 'tis like that in heaven. An angel must travel a bit and talk to people before he amounts to anything. An untraveled angel hasn't a chance up there. The big angels look at him in a funny way. "Bedad," they say "this one's still wet behind the wings."

So O'Ryan kissed his sisters goodby, packed a bit o' lunch, and set off on his great adventure. God must have smiled on him kindly as He watched him go, knowing the love in the tiny cherub's heart. And the Almighty must also have found a great delight in our bold hero, because of the perfection of him.

There are those few, it must be admitted, who will have it only one way: that God was so busy planning a greater delight—not only for heaven but for the world as well—that He had no time to witness the angel's flight. But sure, there's heresy in that—since God knows everything and loves every creature He has made.

Let them quibble who will, there is no doubt of one thing. O'Ryan's heart and soul was filled with the love o' God, and his great intention in visiting the earth was to bring back 'something' to the Lord of Heaven—something that would make God even happier than He was—which was impossible, o' course; but what does an angel know of theology?

"Wurra, wurra," the worried angel said to himself as he came closer and closer to the Emerald Isle. "Now, what would Himself be wanting most from this strange planet? That, I must bring Him."

Scarce had the words said themselves in his mind before he found himself in a bed o' shamrocks, and the lights of a cottage shining in his eyes.

"Men," he said. He flapped his wings for a minute or two, to chase off the dew collected from the shamrocks, and to give himself a dash o' courage. Men were beings he had never seen, and he didn't know how to approach them. But sure, 'twas nothing for him to walk through the walls and into the house as though there were no walls a'tall, a'tall.

And there, in a crib before the fireplace, he saw a *baby*— and him smiling in his sleep. The angel was transformed on the instant by the sight! Never had he seen such strange beauty. Not even in heaven was there anything just like this. 'Twas a beauty all of earth. "Achh, how the good God would enjoy this!" he thought.

And he was just about to carry the baby's smile up with him to highest heaven, when he became aware of the baby's guardian angel. "Scram!" this one said to him. "Be off wit' ya now, ya little omadhoun—b'fore I lose my temper."

O'Ryan was abashed. "I meant no harm, dear sir," He said. "I was just admiring the child, I was. It *is* a child, isn't it? Or maybe it's a woman, or a man?" The ignorance of the cherub softened the big angel; but it didn't amuse him, as it might have amused a man.

"Achh, there now," he said. "I didn't mean to be harsh, nor to be big and important to the likes o' you. No, indeed! But I have a job to do, do ya see? 'Tis I must guard this one, and make a man of him if I can. 'Tis I must send up all his smiles and all his good deeds, all the things God wants most from him. And when he dies, 'tis I must bring his soul to heaven—if heaven be open to him at that time."

He watched the little angel peering about the room with his bright eyes, and took pity on him. With a few quiet words, he put him at ease and gave him the lay o' the land. What's more, he introduced him to the angels who were guarding the child's mother and father. Achh, they had a great gossiping, the four of them, discussing the things of heaven and earth. And as O'Ryan set off for other parts of the world, the baby's guardian angel said a strange thing to him: "Merry Christmas," he said.

O'Ryan pondered that as he flew through the skies, but couldn't make head nor tail of it. He pondered, too, a significant fact: the angels guarding the baby's parents looked old and haggard and thin, though they weren't a second older than the young fella guarding the baby. Sure, and it must be a divil of a job, guarding the earthlings who'd had grown out of their babyhood. The guardian angel of the baby's father had actually grown gray!

But O'Ryan outdistanced these thoughts the farther he flew. 'Twas a fine night; the stars were glorious, and the wind in his face reminded him of the Breath of God. Now, what could he bring God? Maybe the sorrow of a dying sinner sorry for his sins. He'd picked up enough of the Irish angel's lingo to learn about sins and sinners, and God's love for them as they repent, even in the moment of their dying.

But where was he to find a repentant sinner? The Irish said they existed only in Ireland. Nowhere else in the world were there people who sinned so boldly, they said, or repented so violently. Sure, nowhere else in the world did a sinner repent a'tall, a'tall. The situation was so acute in the rest of the world that some of the angels had been talking of a sit-down strike!

"Wurra, wurra," O'Ryan said again and again. 'Twould be a fine thing to find one of those sinners, and his angel on strike. 'Twould be a fine thing to make him repent and bring his clean soul up to Limbo to await *The Happy Day.* "Glory be to God!" he said to himself, all of a sudden. "Merry Christmas—that's what the angel means. Sure 'tis Christmas Eve! And what with the excitement of the trip and all, I clean forgot!"

He looked at the stars, and saw that he still had time to dip down to this country and that in quest of a dying sinner. And this he did, in nation after nation.

In Spain he found a man dying in a palace, with gold pieces all around him, and things hammered and bent and molded out o' gold, and beset with rubies and emeralds and diamonds. But the man's angel was there with him—and he scoffed at the words of the Irish angels.

"Achh, 'tis the way of them all," he told O'Ryan. "The more those angels see of the Irish, the more Irish they themselves become. 'Tis exaggerating, they were, telling you of a sit-down strike. Bedad, there's good and bad in men of all lands, and an angel that knows his business has always a chance. Even with the worst of them, he has a chance. And he never lays down on the job.

"Be off with you now, for I'm in my busiest hour. It wasn't enough that this poor soul given me to guard should be steeped in corruption, but he's steeped in riches too! And it's the gold that's worrying me. It'll drag him down to the deepest pit of hell, if I can't lift the weight of it off him."

O'Ryan looked at the face of the dying sinner, and at the gold. He shrugged his wings. "If I could be of any help . . ." he offered. Not as if he meant it, o' course, but only out of politeness. The other angel shook his head. "Where there's much gold," he said, "only God Himself can be of any help. Be on your way, little one, and a Merry Christmas!"

"The same to you," said O'Ryan, "and many of them." He was over North Africa when he looked at the stars again, and saw that he would have to hurry. And hurry he did. He was still far from the town of Bethlehem when he heard the angel chorus singing of Peace on Earth. But with all his hurry, he stopped to bless himself—like the good Catholic he was.

And then he hurried twice as fast. Sure, he hurried so fast that, what with the friction of the wind and the excitement of getting there on time, he began to shine like a great star. And, as everybody knows, he got there, just above the stable, in the very nick of time, so that his shining glory would do honor to the Child just born.

Never was an angel happier in all eternity, up to this moment, than O'Ryan hovering over the stable in Bethlehem, listening to his fellow angels singing, and watching the shepherds leave their flocks to come and adore. "Glory be to God," he thought to himself, puzzled-like. "I never was happier in heaven itself."

He watched the shepherds go one by one into the stable, and he bade each and every one of them a Merry Christmas.

But they didn't answer him. Sure, and they were bewildered creatures, what with the singing of the angels and the message they had brought to earth, and the splendor of O'Ryan blazing like a great star just overhead. 'Twas dumbfounded they were, besides their bewilderment.

At last there came a shepherd holding a little girl by the hand—a pretty little girl with hair so red that it shone, even in the dark. "Merry Christmas," O'Ryan said to her. He said it a little bashfully, not as he had said it to the men. He had seen men, but until now he had never beheld the beauty of a little girl. So naturally he was bashful. Hearing his voice, the little girl looked up and smiled at him. "Come see the Baby!" she bade him.

Sure, O'Ryan was just waiting for some such invitation, and with no more ado, he dropped down through the roof and hovered over the crib in utter joy and amazement. His little heart fair burst with his great love. And a great hunger and thirst to sing Hosannas was upon him. But alas, he had never learned to sing! He could only adore in silence!

"What's the Baby's name?" the little girl asked the Lady, who was seated in the straw, leaning over the Child and blessing Him with her smile. "His name is *Jesus*," said the Lady.

The angel's heart hammered and hammered inside him as he heard the name. 'Twas such a *beautiful* name! And oh, if those angels outside would only hush up their noise and let him hear the Lady's voice more clearly! Despite his exultation in all he saw and heard, he was vexed with the angelic choir.

How long he remained there, worshiping with all his heart and soul—and feasting his eyes on Mary and Joseph as well as the Baby—O'Ryan himself couldn't have told you. But 'twas soon enough he was out in the cold night with the other angels, and them somewhat disgruntled and unlike themselves. "Glory be to God," O'Ryan said to the choir leader.

"Now why are you so wry-mouthed and glum on such a night?"

"Achh now," said the leader, "leave it to a cherub to ask impertinent questions. If it wasn't Christmas Day itself, divil an answer I'd be giving ya. But, if you must know, there was a sour note somewhere. When the daughter of the shepherd went into the stable, the Son of God cared no more for our music than if we were but the wind, and it hissing like a silly goose. I don't think He listened to us after that."

He strapped his harp comfortably under his left wing, so it wouldn't bother him in the homeward flight. "Now that He's a mortal man, a child is sweeter to Him than all the music we can make."

It wasn't exactly 'grumbling' they were as they shot up to heaven. 'Twas just letting themselves 'talk things out'! And it wasn't altogether unhappy they felt. 'Twas more like a deep puzzlement that was on them, and a sense of having been inadequate somehow.

O'Ryan himself, though no happier angel lived, had no comfort a'tall, a'tall, in the knowledge that he was going back empty-handed to the Throne. Out of all the treasures of earth, he had brought nothing. He had no Christmas Present of any kind for God.

The shame of it began to tear at the overwhelming happiness in his heart. And by the time he stood before the Creator, he could only hang his head.

The singing angels reported all that had happened; and all heaven rejoiced. Never was the music more divine. Never were angels rapt in such ecstasy. Never, it seemed to O'Ryan (peeking through the fingers he had clasped over his eyes), did God's Face shine with such majesty and beauty.

"And there was a little girl with shiny hair," the choir leader said. "I know," God answered. And He beckoned

O'Ryan to come close to Him. "You!" He said. "Tell me what happened in the stable."

"I felt myself in heaven," the wee cherub said simply. "I felt at home. But when the Lady, His sweet mother, told the little girl His name, I would have died of joy—if I could die. His name is *Jesus!*"

At that, all heaven was in a delirium of joy. It doubled and trebled its joy a thousand times. The place rocked with sheer delight. The trumpeter angels blew so loudly into their instruments that they caused tornadoes and whirlwinds and cyclones and wicked storms on earth. The harpists and violinists and piano players and drummers were in such a frenzy of action—on strings and keys and drumheads—that the sun and the moon and all the planets spun 'round in a cosmic dance.

And God reached out and clasped the little angel close to His all-holy breast, and hugged him—so that, angel or not, he swooned away like a chit of a girl. Sure, not even St. Michael himself, prince of all the angels and general of all the armies, had ever such great bliss of God. When he 'came to,' O'Ryan listened almost incredulously to God's praises.

"You have brought Me the greatest gift any angel has ever given Me. You have brought into heaven the greatest joy since heaven is—the name of My Son, Jesus!

"Go you back now, my beloved child; and for your reward, hover brightly over that stable until the wise kings come from the East. Souls you may not bring me, since you are no guardian angel. But men to adore My Son you shall draw, with your shining beauty, from far-off parts." And He kissed the darling angel on the forehead, ere He let him go.

'Tis a story the Irish tell their children, on bright nights in Advent, wherever the Irish be. Yet, bedad, it may have happened just as the Irish tell it, on that lovely night so long ago.

Christmas in Harlem

The last story is true. It is Catherine's account of her expe-
riences one Christmas Eve when she was working at
Friendship House in New York City's Harlem section. "It
will remain one of the mysteries and graces of my life, and
a deeply spiritual one at that," she said. This story is best
read on Christmas Eve at supper time, before Midnight
Mass, for that is when it happened.

It was a sort of upside-down affair that came floating through
my memory when I began to write this story. The memory was
of a Christmas night. It seemed upside down because no one
came through the Blue Door that night in Harlem.

I had just closed it behind the last of our bunch. We had
much to finish up before Midnight Mass. That's when I met
the strange trio that I most assuredly did meet that night.
They did not go through the Blue door but, somehow—and
don't ask me how—the Blue Door was certainly involved.

It was a perfectly natural meeting too, nothing miraculous
about it or about anything that followed. And it was a nice
meeting, one that made Christmas Mass a little more joyous
and the meditations that followed a little more profound.

Just as I was leaving, and had turned from locking the
Blue Door (which had given me some trouble that night I con-
fess—the key stuck or something) I was confronted by a very
handsome Negro man of middle age and a small, younger
woman. Evidently she was his wife, and she was holding a
baby in her arms. I could not see the baby's face. It was all
bundled up against the raw, New York wind that was blowing
into a gale.

Very politely, the man lifted his hat and, in the soft
accents of the deep South, he told me that he and his wife
were lost in this big city. They had just gotten off the train. He

was a carpenter, hoping to get a better job than the one he had in the little village they came from. But, with one thing and another, they had been delayed en route. They didn't have any money—that is, not quite enough for a night's lodging. Perhaps I could tell them where to go, what to do, and to whom they might apply for help.

Having said his piece, he stood relaxed, waiting politely and silently for my answer. His wife, who had never said a word, just smiled once or twice at me. She stood as confident and as still as he, sure that I was just the person to help them.

Before my mind's eye came a vision of the telephone. I almost turned back and opened the Blue Door to try and contact some social agency that would attend to their wants. Then I looked at my wristwatch. It was almost eleven o'clock, and on Christmas Eve!

Whom could I find at this time? And where? And if I did, this poor family would have to brave strange subways. I could, of course, send them by taxi. I did have a few extra dollars in my purse—wonder of wonders. But the 'family shelters' of New York will separate families sometimes, because of lack of room.

Lack of room! Christmas Eve! Man, woman, child! It all suddenly hit me right between the eyes. Of course, I knew it was *just a 'coincidence'!* Nice, in a way. But so many people came to Friendship House just for this kind of help and information.

No, this was not the time to send such a family anywhere. This was the time to offer them personal hospitality, if for no other reason than to atone for the hospitality that was not given almost two thousand years ago.

Of course! Why hadn't I thought of it before? There was what the staff workers of Friendship House called the "Hermitage," that is, my room. It was so many things in one. It had a desk, a bed, a gas stove complete with oven, and a refrigerator, of sorts, given by the management; it even worked sometimes. The room also contained a sink and laundry—a full-grown laundry tub. Yet, all in all, it was a cozy place, especially at night.

I had been given a tinseled Christmas tree about six inches high. It was a far cry indeed from my lofty, native Russian firs, so stately in their majestic beauty. The little tree, nevertheless, was nice, very nice. I had placed under it a miniature crib. When I came back from Mass, I had intended to place the Infant there.

Yes, the room was spick and span, and very, very cozy. Why not invite the couple to spend the night there? Tomorrow I could contact the needed agencies.

No sooner thought than done. My strange couple was still silent, courteously waiting for an answer that surely must have seemed to them a long time in coming. But they showed no sign of impatience.

Slowly, and for some inexplicable reason rather diffidently, I invited them into the hermitage, apologizing for its humbleness and its being many things in one. Their smiles broadened. The woman straightened herself and somehow looked taller as she pressed the child closer to her. The man voiced his thanks and proceeded to follow me.

Thus we walked the three rather long blocks that separated the Blue Door from my quarters. No one said a word. Yet, the silence was companionable.

Once in the room I made them as comfortable as I could. The baby, finally out of its wrappings, was lovely. I had not heard it cry. The man said it was a boy, their firstborn. I made them coffee, fried some eggs, set the table, and then told them I would peek in after Mass.

It was one of the most beautiful Masses I ever participated in. The thought of my three pilgrims snug in their cozy room probably made it so. Personal hospitality to strangers, to

Christ, warms whoever who gives it so much that it is a blessing in itself.

The Mass over, I rushed back to my room. To my astonishment I found the front door ajar! This is *never* done in Harlem, where one uses several locks just in case. (It is the same wherever there are tension, segregation, and poverty.) I pushed the door open. The room was empty.

The dishes had been washed and stacked away, each where it belonged. No signs of occupancy were left whatsoever. The Infant that I had meant to put into its tiny crib under my tinseled tree was already there, and a candle was lit in my window!

Books by Catherine Doherty

Madonna House Classics Series:

Poustinia: Encountering God in Silence, Solitude and Prayer
Sobornost: Experiencing Unity of Mind, Heart and Soul
Strannik: The Call to the Pilgrimage of the Heart
Molchanie: Experiencing The Silence of God
Urodivoi: Holy Fools for The Sake of Christ
Bogoroditza: She Who Gave Birth to God

Other Titles:

Dear Father: A Message of Love to Priests
Dear Parents
Dear Seminarian
Dearly Beloved: Letters to the Children of My Spirit
Donkey Bells: Advent and Christmas
Doubts, Loneliness, Rejection
Fragments of My Life
The Gospel of a Poor Woman
The Gospel Without Compromise
Grace in Every Season
My Russian Yesterdays
Not Without Parables
Season of Mercy: Lent and Easter
Soul of My Soul
Welcome, Pilgrim

If you enjoyed *Donkey Bells*, we think you would also be interested in it's companion volume, *Season of Mercy*:

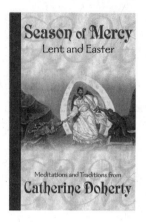

A guide to entering into the mystery and celebration of Lent and Easter!

An inspiring collection of after-dinner talks by Catherine Doherty, spiritual readings around the dining room table—on the spirit, liturgy and customs of Lent, Holy Week, the Easter Triduum and Paschaltide.

"We're in a fantastic world when we're in the world of Lent! We're in the world of repentance, of forgiveness. Now is the moment to repent of our own sins and to forgive everyone."

Grace in Every Season

A rich collection of meditations drawn from the down-to-earth and eminently practical writings of Catherine Doherty. Providing daily spiritual guidance and insights on prayer, this book also includes special reflections for 'Fixed Solemnities, Feasts, and Other Special Occasions.'

"The writings of Catherine Doherty belong in the realm of contemporary classics. With this book of seasonal selections, we have ready-at-hand some of her most memorable reflections on the mysteries of our faith as well as personal accounts of her profound prayer experiences. I heartily recommend it for all Christians."
— Susan Muto, Author, *Pathways to Living*

$14.95 ($18.75 Cdn) • 320 pages • ISBN 0-921440-31-6

Moments of Grace Calendar

This perpetual desktop calendar has a quotation for each day of the year from the writings, diaries, talks and spiritual life of Catherine Doherty. For anyone looking for a deeper insight into the meaning of daily life in Christ, this will provide a new 'Moment of Grace' at home, in the office, or as a gift. It is arranged by date and notes the major feasts and saints' days.

$12.95 ($16.25 Cdn) • 370 pages, 2 color • ISBN 0-921440-56-1

Order toll free: 1-888-703-7110

MADONNA HOUSE PUBLICATIONS
COMBERMERE • ONTARIO • CANADA • K0J 1L0

The aim of our publications is to share the Gospel of Jesus Christ with all people from all walks of life.

It is to awaken and deepen in our readers an experience of God's love in the most simple and ordinary facets of everyday life.

It is to make known to our readers how to live the tender, saving life of God in everything they do and for everyone they meet.

Our publications are dedicated to Our Lady of Combermere, the Mother of Jesus and of His Church, and we are under her protection and care.

Madonna House Publications is a non-profit apostolate of Madonna House within the Catholic Church. Donations allow us to send books to people who cannot afford them but most need them all around the world. Thank you for your participation in this apostolate.

To request a catalogue of our current publications, please call (613) 756-3728, or write to us at:

> Madonna House Publications
> 2888 Dafoe Rd
> Combermere ON   K0J 1L0
> Canada

You can also visit us on the Internet at the following address:

> www.madonnahouse.org